IDIOT'S GUIDE™ TO

the Kama Sutra

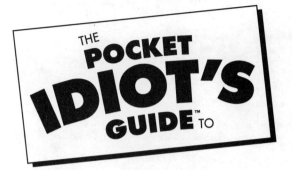

the Kama Sutra

by Ron Louis and David Copeland

ALPHA

A member of Penguin Group (USA) Inc.

ALPHA BOOKS

Published by the Penguin Group

Penguin Group (USA) Inc., 375 Hudson Street, New York, New York 10014, U.S.A.

Penguin Group (Canada), 10 Alcorn Avenue, Toronto, Ontario, Canada M4V 3B2 (a division of Pearson Penguin Canada Inc.)

Penguin Books Ltd, 80 Strand, London WC2R 0RL, England

Penguin Ireland, 25 St Stephen's Green, Dublin 2, Ireland (a division of Penguin Books Ltd)

Penguin Group (Australia), 250 Camberwell Road, Camberwell, Victoria 3124, Australia (a division of Pearson Australia Group Pty Ltd)

Penguin Books India Pvt Ltd, 11 Community Centre, Panchsheel Park, New Delhi—110 017, India

Penguin Group (NZ), cnr Airborne and Rosedale Roads, Albany, Auckland 1310, New Zealand (a division of Pearson New Zealand Ltd)

Penguin Books (South Africa) (Pty) Ltd, 24 Sturdee Avenue, Rosebank, Johannesburg 2196, South Africa

Penguin Books Ltd, Registered Offices: 80 Strand, London WC2R 0RL, England

Copyright © 2004 by Penguin Group (USA) Inc.

All rights reserved. No part of this book shall be reproduced, stored in a retrieval system, or transmitted by any means, electronic, mechanical, photocopying, recording, or otherwise, without written permission from the publisher. No patent liability is assumed with respect to the use of the information contained herein. Although every precaution has been taken in the preparation of this book, the publisher and authors assume no responsibility for errors or omissions. Neither is any liability assumed for damages resulting from the use of information contained herein. For information, address Alpha Books, 800 East 96th Street, Indianapolis, IN 46240.

THE COMPLETE IDIOT'S GUIDE TO and Design are registered trademarks of Penguin Group (USA) Inc.

International Standard Book Number: 1-59257-331-2
Library of Congress Catalog Card Number: 2004113222

06 05 04   8 7 6 5 4 3 2 1

Interpretation of the printing code: The rightmost number of the first series of numbers is the year of the book's printing; the rightmost number of the second series of numbers is the number of the book's printing. For example, a printing code of 04-1 shows that the first printing occurred in 2004.

Printed in the United States of America

Note: This publication contains the opinions and ideas of its authors. It is intended to provide helpful and informative material on the subject matter covered. It is sold with the understanding that the authors and publisher are not engaged in rendering professional services in the book. If the reader requires personal assistance or advice, a competent professional should be consulted.

The authors and publisher specifically disclaim any responsibility for any liability, loss, or risk, personal or otherwise, which is incurred as a consequence, directly or indirectly, of the use and application of any of the contents of this book.

Most Alpha books are available at special quantity discounts for bulk purchases for sales promotions, premiums, fund-raising, or educational use. Special books, or book excerpts, can also be created to fit specific needs.

For details, write: Special Markets, Alpha Books, 375 Hudson Street, New York, NY 10014.

We dedicate this book to all the women who have taught us so much about sexuality and sensuality. We also acknowledge the genius of Vatsyayana. We also thank Dmitri Bilgere and Roan Kaufman without whom this book would not be possible.

Contents

Introduction

Can Ancient Indian secrets make your sex life explode into whole new levels of ecstasy?

The thrilling answer is a resounding *yes*. And even better, these simple sexual secrets are available to you right now.

You don't have to work your way through decoding ancient, obscurely written texts. You don't have to try to imagine what they mean once you find them. We have done the work for you. We've taken the guesswork out of it and created a concise, visual guide to the *Kama Sutra*. You are holding in your hands the result of that work. Make use of it to totally transform your sex life to new levels of physical pleasure and emotional intimacy. It's easy and fun!

Here's what you'll get from this book:

First we'll give you some background on the *Kama Sutra*, and show you how to use this guide, both by yourself and with a partner. Then you'll learn about your body and your partner's body—and some ways of pleasuring each other through simple types of touches that will probably surprise you. You'll learn your partner's erogenous zones and how to electrify those zones to bring your partner extreme pleasure. You'll also learn about the mechanics of sexuality—including birth control and safe sex.

Then you'll discover how to set the sexual mood by creating a romantic and sensual atmosphere. You'll learn how to make the most of romantic details such as the arrangement of the bedroom, the music, sensual scents, and the erotic uses of food.

Once the atmosphere is set, the touching begins. You'll learn the types of passion, and sexual cuddling—an excellent start to a sexual union. Then you'll learn 10 *Kama Sutra* secret ways of kissing—you'll surprise your lover every time with this variety of kissing styles.

Kissing and touching lead to more kissing and touching, so next you'll explore body kissing and oral pleasure, *Kama Sutra* style.

Then you'll discover the basic *Kama Sutra* sexual positions. You'll learn the things the man should do and the things the woman should do to create maximum sexual bliss. You'll get to know the basic and advanced *Kama Sutra* positions, and exactly how to do them. You'll see pictures and read concise descriptions so that you and your partner can start experimenting with the *Kama Sutra* today. You'll learn the surprising value of special starting and ending positions for increasing sexual satisfaction.

And while this book is a guide, we've also provided a "guide for the guide"—special sidebars in each chapter to clarify, simplify, and help you even more as you explore the world of the *Kama Sutra*. These are:

Kama Sutra Words

Definitions of terms used in the *Kama Sutra* and elsewhere.

Sexy Play

Advice on how to make sex better—both from the *Kama Sutra* and from other sources.

Tidbits of Pleasure

Interesting and useful facts about the world of sex and the history of the *Kama Sutra*.

From the Master

Bottom-line quotes from the *Kama Sutra* to help you keep the most important things clearly in mind.

If you want more tips, tricks, and sexual secrets mailed right to your e-mail box, send us at e-mail at tips@passionatekamasutra.com (we will never share your e-mail address with anyone!). Contact the authors directly at authors@passionatekamasutra. com, or visit us on the web at www.passionatekamasutra. com. You can also write us at PO Box 55094, Madison, WI, 53705.

Turn the page, and let's get started!

Ron Louis and David Copeland

Acknowledgments

We would like to thank Gene Brissey, Kirk Bromley, Amy Gile, Steve webmaster for howtosucceedwithwomen.com, Tony Jarvis, Amma, Jen Taylor, Fuzzy H., Atul Mera, Rob, Nicole, Kristin, Darren, Squishy V., Valerie Wyss, R. Fripp, Freddy A., MEO Photo, K. Lasker, M. Kapell, and Hazel for all their support as we created this book. We love you!

Trademarks

All terms mentioned in this book that are known to be or are suspected of being trademarks or service marks have been appropriately capitalized. Alpha Books and Penguin Group (USA) Inc. cannot attest to the accuracy of this information. Use of a term in this book should not be regarded as affecting the validity of any trademark or service mark.

Taking the Path of Sexual Ecstasy

In This Chapter

- The history of the *Kama Sutra*
- How to modify positions to work with your specific body
- The four paths to loving

In 1883, an English adventurer, linguist, and writer named Richard Burton self-published the first English translation of a 2,000-year-old Sanskrit text dedicated to the art of sexual pleasure and spiritual development entitled *Kama Sutra*. While the prudish moral code of Victorian England prevented the book from major distribution, the sexual revolution of the 1960s brought new interest in its sensual wisdom. Today, the

Kama Sutra is one of the most well-known and widely read books in the world.

Kama Sutra comes from two Sanskrit words, meaning rules *(kama)* of love *(sutra)*. *Kama Sutra* can also be translated as "Sayings of Passion" or "Aphorisms of Desire." No matter the exact English meaning of the phrase, the *Kama Sutra* is a detailed guidebook, among other things, on how a couple can achieve a richer, fuller, more mutually satisfying sex life together.

The *Kama Sutra* is actually a compilation of different texts, and a man named Vatsyayana is generally considered to be the one responsible for the compiling. These various texts were probably written records of an oral tradition of instructional verse that was passed down from generation to generation in India in the first 500 years C.E. Though we don't know for sure when the *Kama Sutra* was put to paper, experts believe it was somewhere around 400 or 500 C.E.

In many ways the world in which the *Kama Sutra* was created was much different than the one in which we currently live. Ancient India was a place of strict social castes, gender inequality, and polygamy. In one way, however, their world was the same as ours: Men and women loved having great sex together. And it is a testament to the quality of the advice in the *Kama Sutra* that it is still used today by couples looking to share more fun in bed.

The staying power of the *Kama Sutra* is unparalleled not only due to its significance in the history of sexuality, but also its applicability to modern sexuality and its applications in the bedroom that span over centuries. Even though it was compiled in an age of inequality, it is deeply committed to both partners achieving satisfaction from sexual union. And by reading the *Kama Sutra* rather than, say, some newer text on "how to have great sex," you not only gain access to an ancient, time-tested art of eroticism, but you also benefit from the spiritual lessons offered by the book—the *Kama Sutra* enlightens your mind so that you can enjoy your body and the body of your partner.

At its heart the *Kama Sutra* represents a code of conduct. It not only makes suggestions on how to enjoy sex, but it states clearly that enjoying sex is a responsibility. Couples owe it to themselves to learn the positions and pleasure techniques described in the *Kama Sutra*. By embracing the "rules of love" and following them closely and joyously, a couple can significantly enhance their love life and enjoy one another with ever greater passion and intimacy.

How to Get the Most from This Book

You will benefit from perusing the *Kama Sutra* whether you currently have a lover or not.

Practicing Alone

If you are between lovers right now, the *Kama Sutra* can still be of great benefit to you, for three reasons:

- You will be better prepared when you do find a lover. We suggest you read over the descriptions of a position, look at the pictures, and really take some time to imagine yourself with a lover, getting into and making love in that position. Reread the tips about the position while you do this. Actually imagine feeling a lover's body against yours in that position; imagine the adjustments that both of you might have to make to really get into the position comfortably. Also imagine performing the details of the transitions from one position to another.

  When you do get a lover, these "mental practice sessions" will help you easily and smoothly introduce and practice *Kama Sutra* sex, even if you've never done it before.

- Studying the *Kama Sutra* increases your sexual confidence, which makes you more relaxed and attractive to a potential lover. Mastering the *Kama Sutra* gives you a secret "sexual edge" over other possible lovers. This confidence will help you both in the bedroom and when you interact socially with the opposite sex—which will, in turn, make them more likely to want to become your lover.

- Studying the *Kama Sutra* is fun! By all means, pleasure yourself when you imagine being in the positions. Imagine being with an ideal lover as you fantasize about using the *Kama Sutra*, step by step. The more pleasure you can bring yourself, while still learning the precise details of each of the sexual postures, the better prepared you'll be when your next lover does show up in your life.

Practicing with Your Lover

While studying the *Kama Sutra* alone is informative, useful, and fun, your sex life will really flower when you practice it in partnership with a lover.

Many couples exploring the *Kama Sutra* find it easier to first look at the guide when they are not in bed, and you may want to try this, too. Look at the pictures together, and read the instructions for the position aloud to each other.

Talk about things that might work for you both about the position, and possible pitfalls or difficulties you might have with it. Lack of sufficient flexibility is the main problem couples have. Brainstorm modifications you might use, before you go to the bedroom. Also think about what posture might follow or precede the position you are investigating. The *Kama Sutra* is a menu of sexual options. What might you want to try today?

When you are being sexual together, take another look at this guide, and start trying out the positions you studied.

Making Modifications

As with the rest of life, you will do much better with the *Kama Sutra* if you practice it with open communication and with a sense of humor. This is not like construction work or factory labor, even though there are precise instructions and a goal in mind. Practicing the *Kama Sutra* is not a grim job, and each moment of it is not a serious responsibility!

Open communication is critical. For instance, following the instructions of the *Kama Sutra* should never hurt. If it does start to hurt, say something!

More often, however, you will simply find yourself unable to stretch your body into the described position—in fact, some of the postures will be too difficult for people who aren't advanced yoga practitioners. Tell your partner when this happens. Most of the positions can be modified by using pillows or low tables for support. We'll tell you how to make those modifications in the descriptions of the positions.

Tell your partner when a position isn't working for you, and experiment with the modifications. Don't worry if you lose the "sexual mood" while you are talking about and making these adjustments. Remember, practicing the *Kama Sutra* is not a race! Relax, be together, touch each other's bodies, and don't pressure yourself to "do it right." If you don't get into the position this time, do something else and come back to it in a future lovemaking session When practicing the *Kama Sutra*, the only failure is pressuring yourself to "do it right," and ruining the fun.

Also allow yourself to have a sense of humor. Funny, unexpected things will happen as you start getting into the positions. Approach this with a light heart, and be willing to laugh!

The Four Paths to Loving

The *Kama Sutra* says that love takes four forms, or follows four paths, as it grows between two people. These paths are imagination, practice, belief, and objects. If a man and a woman only share one or two of these paths, their relationship will be less than ideal. To share in and travel down all these paths is to experience erotic fulfillment. Here is a listing of the four paths to loving:

- **Love resulting from imagination.** A love relationship begins with imagination. Each lover imagines, or fantasizes, about the other, often picturing or internally desiring acts of love that neither would actually ever do. By imagining possible sexual activities, partners become excited by and open to one another's bodies.

- **Love acquired by practice.** From imagination, lovers move on to practice. Engaging in the realization of their imaginations, a man and woman begin to share preferences for kinds of lovemaking. By practicing these sexual activities, the couple grows closer, more intimately aware of each other's desires and potential for bliss.

- **Love acquired through belief.** Belief refers to the deepening of the relationship into realms of commitment and bonding.

You begin to feel at home with each other. A sense of belonging, of partnership, and a belief in the other person develops. In this stage, the bond between a man and a woman grows more intense, and this increased emotional intensity can lead to even more intense lovemaking.

- **Love resulting from objects.** Finally, the *Kama Sutra* sees objects as a part of a successful union. If she wants a huge house, three cars, and a 20-foot yacht, and he wants to live the life of a hermit, problems are going to occur. While modern romantics might think such concerns beneath them, most of us know it to be true—a man and a woman that are constantly arguing over money are going to have a hard time achieving harmony in the sack.

Imagination, practice, belief, and a mutual desire for objects—when all of these take place in the proper manner, lovers can be joined at a deep and mutually arousing level. Great sex isn't just about getting physical. It's about having all the spiritual elements lined up as well. By imagining, practicing, believing in, and sharing object-desires with your lover, your sex life will grow richer and more satisfying.

The Least You Need to Know

- The *Kama Sutra* is a 2,000-year-old Sanskrit text about "the rules of love," brought to the west in 1883 and popular ever since.

- You will benefit from studying the *Kama Sutra* whether or not you currently have a sexual partner.

- When you practice with your lover, look at the pictures together, read the text aloud, and imagine what modifications you might need to make for your body types.

- The *Kama Sutra* is not meant to be painful or difficult, so if you can't get into a position during a lovemaking session, don't worry— just try it again next time.

Chapter 2

Understanding the Body

In This Chapter

- Understanding the male body
- Understanding the female body
- Erogenous Zones
- Birth control methods

Before we move into the sexy stuff we need to cover some basic information about men and women. The *Kama Sutra* teaches a system of sensual pleasure, but it does not cover the actual biology and anatomy of male and female bodies. We have found that having a basic understanding of the body is very important in pleasuring yourself and your partner. In this chapter, we look at the physical world of men and women and deepen our understanding of pleasuring our bodies.

Men 101

Let's start by looking at the anatomy of the man. The male body can be confusing because so much of male sexuality is based on stimulation to the penis. We often forget there are other erotic spots and other options for sexual and sensual contact.

The Three Different Types of Men

According to the *Kama Sutra*, there are three kinds of men: the Hare Man, the Bull Man, and the Stallion Man. The distinction not only describes the length of each type of man's *lingam* and the type of *yoni* best matched to it, but also characteristics of each type's personality.

Kama Sutra Words

In the *Kama Sutra*, the penis is called the **lingam** and the vagina is called the **yoni**. We'll use these terms throughout the rest of this book.

The three kinds of men are:

- **The Hare Man.** The hare man has a penis that is about three inches in length when erect. The best type of yoni for such a lingam is that of the doe, shallow and narrow. The Hare Man's body is small and lively and his demeanor and voice are gentle and pleasant.

- **The Bull Man**. This kind of man has a thick lingam that is approximately four inches long when erect. A full and sensuous mare yoni best matches this lingam. The Bull Man has a robust and hearty temperament and a powerful presence.

- **The Stallion Man.** The stallion man has a lingam that is around six inches when erect and it is best suited to the spacious and deep elephant yoni. He is tall, muscular, and savors adventure.

No two men are identical, and each man is best suited to a particular kind of woman. Finding your match is a key component to achieving a passionate sex life.

Erogenous Zones for Men

Erogenous zones are pleasure spots: areas of the body that turn you on when they are touched. Erogenous zones often are areas of the body we don't commonly associate as sensual spots, so listen up.

Although most men tend to be shy about admitting it, their bodies are covered with sensual spots. Women, here's a listing of a few erogenous zones to try on your man tonight. You can also make up your own and use them during any phase of the lovemaking process.

- **Scalp.** The scalp can be an erogenous zone for men. If you've got long nails, try gently scratching his scalp, or give him a sensual head massage.

- **Neck.** Another hot spot on a man, which is not usually associated with sensuality, is his neck. You can stroke it gently with your fingertips, kiss it gently, or touch it with different parts of your body.

- **Ears.** Most men have ultra-sensitive ears. You can drive him wild by whispering softly into his ears and then nibbling on his lobes. Nibble lightly, and suck and blow gently into and around his ears.

- **Fingers.** Giving a man a hand massage is a great way to relax him. There are hundreds of nerve endings in the hand.

- **Chest.** A man's chest is another greatly overlooked erotic zone. Many men have highly sensitive nipples that respond well to kissing, sucking, and squeezing. And then you've got his upper chest and, of course, the treasure trail leading down towards his lingam. Rub the entire area gently and slowly.

- **Back.** Who doesn't love a good back rub? After a long day, a nice back rub is the perfect way to help your man relax and transition into playtime with you.

  Start at his shoulders with gentle caresses and work your way down. Move slowly and steadily, and he will be putty in your hands.

- **Buttocks.** Men love their buttocks touched and stroked. It's one of the turn-on areas on his body that is often ignored during massage and during lovemaking. Soft gentle strokes are great to start with. A nice butt rub can be a good transition activity from the nonerotic to the erotic.

- **Thighs.** Men's thighs can be surprisingly sensitive. It's important to be gentle and to use steady movements. You can also gently blow on his legs as you nibble his thighs. Be careful though—he might be ticklish (but that could be fun in itself!).

The Male Sex Spots

Now let's discuss the common sex spots on a man: his scrotum and penis.

Sexy Play

Yes, men have the equivalent of a G-spot, similarly to women. The male G-spot is his prostate gland. Numerous nerve bundles pass by the prostate on their way to the penis, thus making it a pleasure center for men.

There are two ways to find the G-spot. The first way is to use a lubricated finger to enter the anus and press toward the front of his body. You can find it because it feels like a small rounded walnut size lump. You can then rub and massage it, to his great pleasure.

The second option allows you to find the male G-spot without entering the anus. A woman can rub the man's perineum (the area between the anus and the scrotum) and get much of the same effect.

Spotlight on the Scrotum

The scrotum is the pouch that covers the testicles. This is also a very erotic and sensitive area on a

man's body. Many men love to have their testicles massaged and rubbed during sex play. Start
gently! When we say this area is sensitive, we
mean it!

The Penis/Lingam

We would be committing a major faux paux if
we didn't provide some basic information about
the penis, or lingam. The erectile tissue of the
penis consists of two parallel cylindrical compo-
nents: the *corpus cavernosa* near to top of the
penis and, underneath, the *corpus spongiosum*
through which passes the urethra. The glans,
located at the tip of the penis, is covered with
a thinner, more sensitive skin than the shaft of
the penis.

In later chapters, we will discuss lingam massage
techniques as well as oral sex techniques.

Male Orgasm

We tend to associate male orgasm with ejaculation, but this is only one aspect of the male
orgasm process. Some of the stages of male
orgasm include the penis increasing in length,
width, and rigidity. His testes enlarge by 50
to 100 percent of their normal size. A man's
blood pressure also shoots up; his heart rate

accelerates, as does his breathing rate. Next, his body becomes tense. His face tightens, his hands clasp, and his toes curl. His nipples harden. His brain is also swamped with sensations of pleasure. Nearing ejaculation, his skin flushes with blood, causing his body to redden.

Women 101

Now let's shift gears and explore the basic anatomy of women. If you are a man, this section may help you understand your lover's body. If you are a woman, this section is especially for the confused male in your life.

The Three Kinds of Women

The *Kama Sutra* describes three categories of women: the Deer (or Doe) Woman, the Mare Woman, and the Elephant Woman. As with men, these categories not only apply to the type of yoni possessed by that class of woman, but it also says something about her temperament. Here are the three kinds of women:

- **The Deer or Doe Woman.** This type of woman has a petite frame and a gentle manner. Her yoni is tight and shallow, making her best suited to the smaller lingam of the Hare Man.

- **The Mare Woman.** The mare woman is stout of body, and her look and personality are a little on the wild side. Her yoni is full and sensuous, so she is most suited to the Bull Man.

- **The Elephant Woman.** This type of woman is big-boned and tall, her complexion is radiant, and she is harmonious of demeanor. With a deep and wide yoni, she is best matched with the Stallion Man.

Erogenous Zones for Women

Just as men have erogenous zones, so do women. These are important pleasure centers to touch, massage, kiss, and pay attention to in any aspect of lovemaking.

- **Wrists.** A woman's wrists can be a major pleasure center. Use a very light touch. Some women also enjoy it when a man nuzzles or nibbles the insides of her wrists.

- **Ears.** Many women enjoy having their ears licked, sucked, or kissed. Although blowing in their ears is acceptable, it's not what women enjoy most. Most women enjoy having you whisper sweet nothings in their ears; you can also whisper sweet compliments and sexy thoughts.

- **Feet.** After a hard day at work, what woman doesn't like a foot rub? A few options include an oil massage or soaking her feet in hot water before a massage. For the most relaxing experience, you should take your time rubbing her feet. Make sure to rub the soles of her feet, her toes, and her ankles.

- **Hair and scalp.** Rubbing a woman's head is a great way to start a massage. Start out gently. Rubbing a woman's scalp is deeply relaxing and can be a great way to transition from a busy day to the peaceful and safe time of lovemaking.

    We also recommend gently stroking the woman's hair. This is especially erotic for women with long hair.

- **Nape of the neck.** The neck is the perfect sensual spot on a woman's body. It looks sexy, and is the gateway to so much pleasure. For relaxation purposes, a neck rub is perfect. It relaxes her entire head, as well as her shoulders and chest. Men: If you lover is stressed, try rubbing her neck.

    Simply breathing on a woman's neck can give her goose bumps all over—and try using your tongue or teeth to get her aroused.

- **Behind the knees.** Everyone's knees are sensitive. The area behind the knees is an erogenous zone because of the many nerve endings there. Many women find it a blissful experience to have this area stroked, kissed, or nibbled on.

- **Inner thighs.** Where to go next from the knees? How about the inner thighs? This area can be quite erotic because it leads to the yoni. As a result, the inner thighs are highly sensitive to touching, stroking, and licking. For men, remember that the inner thighs are the gateway to passion!

- **Buttocks.** The buttocks and the lower back of a woman are major erotic zones. Conveniently, men find this area of a woman irresistible. Touching the woman's buttocks is usually a win-win proposition for a couple.

  Rubbing the buttocks will turn a woman on, as well as relax her. Some women also enjoy having their buttocks firmly grabbed. However, negotiating the intensity of touch is probably a good idea.

The Female Sex Spots

Now let's discuss the common sex spots on a woman: her breasts, vagina, clitoris, and G-spot.

Breasts

The breasts are very sexually sensitive, and many women find it deeply pleasurable when they are touched. We probably don't need to say this, but we recommend the man fondle, lick, and massage his lover's breasts and nipples. Be gentle at first when touching the breasts. Simply trace their shape, explore them, and increase intensity if the woman is enjoying it.

Vagina/Yoni

The vulva is the external female genitalia, including the clitoris and the inner and outer labia surrounding the urethral and vaginal openings. The labia major are the outer lips of the vagina, and the inner lips are called the labia minor.

The cervix is the lower portion of the uterus, which opens to the vagina. The cervix is high up and at the end of the vaginal canal, so it is not visable or external, as the labia are.

Clitoris

The labia minora meet to form small folds at the top of the vulva, just above the clitoris. The external tip, or glans, of the clitoris is the part of a woman's genitals most sensitive to touch. The clitoris also has two internal legs that straddle each side of the vagina. The inner lips join together to form the hood of the clitoris.

The clitoris is made of spongy tissue, much like the tissue of the penis—full of nerve endings and blood vessels. During sexual arousal, blood flow increases, and the clitoris swells and becomes firmer.

Believe it or not, biologically, the clitoris is equivalent to the male penis. That's right, for the first few months after conception, the genitalia of the male and female are exactly the same.

The G-Spot

Most women have a difficult time finding their own G-Spot. It's much easier to have your partner find it with you. The G-Spot is located along the upper/front wall of the vagina, about two inches in, toward the stomach. Try some manual exploration. Lie on your back on the floor with your knees bent and rest your feet on the bed in front of you. You or your partner insert a finger into the yoni and gently stroke the front wall behind the pubic bone, about two inches up. He should feel a patch of skin that has a different texture from the rest of the vaginal walls, slightly rough. If he uses a forward motion pressing into the center of this ruffled patch until he hits an area that is sensitive to pressure. This area is the G-Spot, also known as your urethral sponge. It's on the other side of your vaginal wall, which is why you'll probably respond more to pressure than light stroking. The area is about the size of a pea, but can enlarge to the size of a walnut when stimulated.

Female Orgasm

When a woman is reaching orgasm, her central nervous system sends signals to her heart so that it starts beating more rapidly. Her adrenaline flow shoots up, which expands her arteries, sending more blood to her sex centers. Her breathing rate also increases, allowing her to better oxygenate her blood.

When a woman orgasms, she feels a sudden, intense blissful sensation, her breasts enlarge, her nipples become erect, her vaginal fluids flow more freely, her pelvic muscles contract rhythmically, and she usually makes sounds of pleasure. If she has multiple orgasms, these reactions will occur over a longer period of time, in waves that peak, dip, peak, and

so on. If the orgasm occurs primarily through clitoral stimulation, it is usually described as *sharper.* If
it occurs primarily through G-spot stimulation, it is
usually described as *deeper.*

Birth Control Methods

The *Kama Sutra* is all about options. It's all about
having exposure to a wide variety of positions and
ideas so that you can openly communicate with
your partner and create the sex life—and the
relationship—of your dreams. An important part
of sexuality and intimacy is discussing birth control
and understanding the options.

Whether you're interested in getting pregnant or
not, we strongly believe you should be in agreement
with your partner before making any decisions of
this magnitude. Therefore, we want to make sure
you understand the various forms of birth control
and some of their advantages and disadvantages.
We'll now discuss several birth control options,
we will then look at how to prevent STDs.

Condoms

Condoms are the easiest to use, and one of the least
expensive types of birth control. We recommend
you buy condoms that contain spermicide. Always
use latex condoms, because lambskin condoms

don't block HIV and other STDs. Do not use polyurethane condoms, because they tend to break more often than latex.

Spermicide

There are many types of spermicide. They are all available over the counter at most drugstores. A few types include a cream, foam, jelly, or an insert that is placed in the vagina. Experts recommend that you use spermicide with other forms of birth control.

Other Methods of Birth Control

You and your partner need to discuss which form(s) of birth control works best for you. You can get the following forms from your doctor: diaphragm, cervical cap, the pill, morning after pill, I.U.D., Norplant, and Depo Provera.

Safe Sex Tips

Following the *Kama Sutra* path means keeping yourself healthy, happy, and following safe sex guidelines. In fact, practicing safe sex is important for all couples. Safe sex means making sure you don't get anyone else's blood, semen, or vaginal fluids in your body—and protecting your partners, too!

Prevention of STDs

While it is normal and healthy for people to enjoy active sex lives, there are more than 30 sexually transmitted diseases (STDs) and sexually transmitted infections (STIs) that can make your life unpleasant. Every year millions of people in the United States get STDs. Nobody is immune. Practice safe sex so you won't have to worry about STDs and STIs, and sex will be a lot more fun.

As we mentioned, condoms are the only way to protect yourself and your partner from STDs and HIV—but they're not foolproof. You've got to use them correctly every time you have sex.

Preventing HIV

Unsafe sex brings with it a high risk of spreading HIV. The greatest risk is when blood or sexual fluid touches the soft, moist areas (mucous membrane) inside the rectum, vagina, mouth, or at the tip of the penis. These areas can be damaged easily, which gives HIV a way to get into the body.

To protect yourself from HIV and STDs, always use a condom in addition to other forms of birth control.

Safer Oral Sex

There is the risk of being infected with HIV "in having unprotected oral sex with a man or a woman; however, it is not as risky as unprotected anal or vaginal sex. HIV is found in: blood, breast milk, semen, and vaginal fluids. The virus can be transmitted through: cuts, mucous membranes (anus, mouth, vagina), openings, and sores.

During oral sex, to avoid risk of HIV infection, it is important to keep semen and vaginal fluids out of your mouth. It's also important to make sure that your mouth is healthy and you do not have bleeding gums, cuts, or mouth sores, as the presence of blood will increase your risk.

To keep vaginal fluids out of your mouth when having oral sex with a woman, use: a dental dam or a piece of plastic wrap as a barrier between the mouth and the vagina. Along with dental dams, the latex face mask can be worn to protect the one who is giving oral stimulation to their partner. These masks are worn over the mouth and are designed to make it easier to give oral sex.

To keep semen out of your mouth when having oral sex with a man, use a latex condom.

The Least You Need to Know

- Men and women are different, and the *Kama Sutra* recognizes their differences.

- Part of your job as a *Kama Sutra* master is to understand how your body and your partner's body works.

- Touching erogenous zones is a critical part of making love, relaxing your partner, aiding in the transition into other sensual contact, and enhancing lovemaking.

- Safe sex is crucial when making love.

Setting the Mood

In This Chapter

- How to make your bedroom a sensual paradise
- Sensual foods
- Sensual music
- The art of sensual talk

The *Kama Sutra* speaks often about the importance of having a romantic environment. Vatsyayana explains that, "The *Kama Sutra* is the enjoyment of appropriate objects by the five senses of hearing, feeling, seeing, tasting, and smelling, assisted by the mind together with the soul." In other words, when you practice the *Kama Sutra*, you are not just practicing sex positions—you are exploring a complete system of sensuality.

The trick is to make your bedroom and your home reflect that sense of sensuality in your everyday life. This chapter teaches you how to do that.

The Art of Arranging the Bedroom

Let's start by talking about creating a romantic bedroom environment. If your bedroom is neat and relaxing, it will be more conducive for sex. If, on the other hand, your bedroom is messy, smelly, and cluttered, it will be a lot harder to fan the fires of passion.

Creating the Vibe

Think of the bedroom as your *Kama Sutra* work-shop. In your workshop you need to have your props; you need the space to be clear of distractions and clutter; and you need the space to make it easy to do your job as a romantic *Kama Sutra*–love pro. You will use your workshop to create more pleasure between your partner and yourself than you can possibly stand.

Cleanliness

Your first job is to get every nonessential item out of the bedroom. This means putting away the junk and getting the unpacked boxes out of the corners. It also means that you might want to remove your computer, exercise equipment, and anything else that does not belong in a romantic space. Then vacuum, mop, dust, and make the place spotless.

Flooring

Romance is in the details, and one of the details is your bedroom floor. Therefore, you better make sure the floor is nice. Carpets that are of a light pastel color make a room more open and airy. If you have a hardwood floor, you may want to add an area rug or, for the ultimate in romance, a Persian or bear rug. Remember, you may end up making love on the floor—so you want it to be inviting.

Artwork

Look at the artwork on your bedroom walls. Does it put you in a romantic mood? If it doesn't, replace it. We recommend you hang art that communicates personally to you. If you enjoy watercolors, oil paintings, photography, and so on, then put them on your walls! You can also hang tapestries or textiles to bring color and texture to your room.

Flowers

Flowers are mentioned throughout the *Kama Sutra* as a way to adorn any room. Flowers create both a visually, as well as aromatically, appealing room.

People have personal preferences, but for most people roses are the most romantic flower, with daises and tulips coming in second and third.

Curtains

Lush curtains and window treatments can be an incredibly romantic and sensual decorating aspect of your room. Think of an ideal romantic relationship scene with your partner, and then think of what style and color curtains complement that scene.

The Bed

You need a bed that is large, soft, and inviting. This means at least queen size, but we prefer the king-size bed. Some people find canopy style beds romantic, while others prefer the classic waterbed. No matter what you prefer, find one that when you lay in it you feel like a king or a queen.

Satin, silk, or high-thread-count cotton sheets are required if you want to make your bed into a true love zone. The soft sheets tend to hug your body and make you feel special.

We recommend you get either a down or feather comforter. Remember, you want your bedroom to feel lush and opulent. If there's one place to go "all-out," it's with the bedclothes.

You also should have plenty of pillows. They can be used to help hold you in different positions, and that can make all the difference.

Here is an arrangement of pillows we suggest: At least four or five standard or queen-size pillows, six or more various-size pillows, and at least two large pillows for sitting on the floor—or for pillow fights!

Soft Lighting

No one in their right mind feels sensual in a brightly lit room. Try soft, reflected light. You can get special lights, or simply replace your 100-watt bulbs with 40-watts, or you can also turn off the lights entirely and let light come in from the next room.

Nothing says romance like a candle-lit room. A candle-lit bedroom full of pillows, with soft romantic music playing, is irresistible.

For an alternative you can try aromatic candles. Aromatic candles have calming and aphrodisiac qualities. You can also play with the colors, height, texture, style, and grouping of your candles. Each change creates a different effect. We recommend having many candles in the bedroom for love-making sessions. Just be sure to put them out before you go to sleep, and never leave candles unattended!

Music

Good music is completely subjective. Everyone has his or her own musical preferences. If you explore enough, you will find the music that is perfect for you and your lovemaking.

Try some of these:

Classical:

- Rachmaninov, Piano Concerto no. 1, second movement, Piano Concerto no. 2, second movement.
- Mozart, piano Concerto no. 21 in C, second movement
- Pachelbel, Canon in D major
- Mahler, Symphony no. 5, Adagietto movement

New Age and Trance:

- Enya
- Delerium
- Tangerine Dream
- Deep Forest
- Sacred Spirit
- Vangelis
- Dead Can Dance
- Peter Gabriel "passion" CD

Movie Soundtracks:

- *Casino*
- *Good Morning Vietnam*
- *The Big Blue*
- *Braveheart*
- Soundtracks to Quentin Tarantino movies such as *Pulp Fiction*

Jazz/Soul:

- Luther Vandross
- Miles Davis
- Frank Sinatra
- Barry White
- Marvin Gaye

Scents and Sensuality

Smell is incredibly powerful. It works subconsciously in your brain to draw up forgotten feelings and to set—or destroy—moods. In fact, 99 percent of animals are driven by subconscious pheromones. Men, especially, tend to forget the importance of the proper smells in lovemaking.

It's important to have pleasant, erotic smells in the bedroom. And it's equally important to get rid of anything in the bedroom that smells like old sweat socks (or worse). Check with your partner and make sure any scent you plan to use is a scent they enjoy. Otherwise you can kill the mood, rather than create it.

Here is a list of oils to try:

- Ambrete Seed (spicy/musky scent)
- Chamomile (fruity scent)
- Cinnamon (spicy)
- Ginger (spicy)
- Jasmine (floral)
- Lavender
- Patchouli (woodsy)
- Myrrh (calming)
- Rose
- Sandalwood (woodsy)
- Vanilla
- Ylang-Ylang

Foods to Get You in the Mood

Food and sex is a great combination, if you do it right. Remember to avoid messy foods such as corn chips (a lot of crumbs), or nachos (cheese sauce on the blanket). Instead, focus on two groups of foods in the bedroom: fruits and sweets.

Fruits:

- Strawberries (also with whipped cream, or chocolate covered, or champagne soaked)
- Grapes
- Banana slices
- Kiwi slices
- Cherries

Sweets:

- Chocolates
- Cheesecake
- Hershey's Kisses
- Jelly beans
- Marshmallows
- M&M's
- Chocolate covered raisins
- Chocolate truffles
- Bon bons

Note: Do not use any of these inside the vagina! The woman's body maintains a certain acid/alkaline balance in the vagina, and anything with sugar in it (including fruit) can mess up that balance and contribute to yeast infections. You have been warned!

The Art of Sensual Talk

You've prepared the bedroom. You've cleaned, organized, and focused on the details. You have sensual scents, music, and food. And you are enjoying all this together.

The next step is romantic and sensual talk. A romantic, sensual conversation can often act as a form of foreplay, and act as a transition between day-to-day activities and romantic activities.

To start, sensual talk requires an "indoor voice." In other words, talk quietly, almost at a whisper. Get close. This will keep the mood mellow and relaxed.

Give Compliments

Giving and receiving compliments is crucial in a relationship. A good compliment exposes yourself to your partner and makes you a little vulnerable by taking a risk. That means complimenting your lover on what you love most about her, or on what you appreciate most about being with her.

When you're in the heat of passion, it's always good to compliment your partner on her technique. This will boost her confidence and let her know you appreciate what she's doing and motivate her to do it more.

Share About Sexuality

One of the most important—and most erotic—things to talk about is what you like and dislike sexually. This is important information for both of you to share and know about each other.

Sexual fantasies are another good topic of discussion. Sharing about fantasies helps create sexual excitement and trust, and to open up honest communication between partners. It's best to take turns sharing desires and fantasies. You can then hopefully transition into acting out some of them.

Topics to Avoid in Bed

While some topics will bring the two of you together, others will do quite the opposite. These topics are best avoided in the bedroom. Avoid talking about mundane topics when you're in bed. In other words, leave work at work. And specifically avoid negative topics—the news, problems at work, family issues, or anything else that invokes a sense of doom and gloom.

Other Enhancements

While talking to your partner it's important to focus on smiling. Yes, a big smile is always inviting and lovely.

Eye contact is also an important element in talking to your partner. This isn't a staring contest, rather a relaxed gentle look that can have your partner know you are focusing on her.

Casual touch can also assist in connecting you with your partner. Little touches when talking, such as brushing your hand against your partner, touching her face, or reaching over to touch her, all convey comfort, trust, and openness.

The Least You Need to Know

- Sensuality at it's best involves stimulating all five senses: touch, taste, sight, smell, and sound.
- The layout and design of your bedroom is really important in creating a romantic feel.
- It's important to make sure your partner likes any scents you use in the bedroom.
- Sweet conversations are another important part of a romantic experience.

Chapter 4

The Perfect Embrace

In This Chapter

- The three types of passion
- Sensual massage
- Tips for men on massaging women
- Tips for women on massaging men

The *Kama Sutra* shows how the embrace can become a particularly potent lovemaking tool. In fact, embracing is seen as such an important part of arousal that it can take you to places not even the *Kama Sutra* itself can describe, "The whole subject of embracing is of such a nature that men who ask questions about it, or who talk about it, acquire thereby a desire for enjoyment."

The Three Types of Passion

It might be hard to believe, but not everyone feels ready for sex at all times of the day and night. Passion varies, even among the most lascivious members of our society. And the *Kama Sutra* is careful to point out that the best sexual unions occur between equally passionate partners.

The three kinds of passion are described in descending order of force:

- **Intense.** For those with intense passion, sex is thrilling and deeply sensuous.
- **Middling.** For those with middling passion, sex is a generally good time but nothing to write home about.
- **Feeble.** For those with feeble passion, sex is about as exciting as putting on your socks.

The best unions occur between those of equal passion force. Intense with intense, for instance, is described as a High Union. When Intense pairs with Middling, this is a Low Union. When Intense pairs with Feeble, this is a Very Low Union, otherwise known as a big bummer.

Finding the right mix that keeps your passion force predominantly in the intense range is what the art of the *Kama Sutra* is all about.

The Joys of Massage

What better way to start *embracing* than massage? We're now going to discuss massage techniques, from soothing to erotic. This will start you out in the "embracing" sort of mood and build toward all out sensual embrace.

> **Kama Sutra Words**
>
> The *Kama Sutra* refers to **embrace** to indicate any touching of bodies between a man and a woman that leads to, or occurs during sex. An embrace is a way to signify sexual interest or enhance sexual activity. By embracing, a couple puts their energies in sync and expresses or intensifies their passions.

Soothing Massage

Soothing massages are meant to relax, entice, and to relieve muscle tension. There are four kinds of hand motions to use when giving a soothing massage.

- **Stroking.** In this type of massage, muscles are lightly grabbed and lifted, and then stroked. This kind of massage is a good way to start the process.

- **Friction.** You do this type of massage by using thumbs and fingertips to work in deep circles into the thickest part of muscles.

- **Tapotement.** This sort of massage means chopping, beating, and tapping strokes on your beloved. This type of massage also includes taking your fingers and pressing or flattening them firmly on a muscle, and then the area is shaken rapidly for a few seconds.

- **Rocking.** This sort of massage employs gentle, rocking massage to help release stress and tension.

Sexy Play

The significance of breathing techniques as it applies to the *Kama Sutra* is that breathing techniques help you to relax, focus, and connect more deeply with your partner during lovemaking.

Deep breathing helps to facilitate relaxation and calm intense emotional states. Deep breathing slows you down and provides more oxygen to your body, whereas shallow breathing leads to increased anxiety and stress.

Here's one basic technique: Begin by breathing normally, but paying attention to each breath. After several breaths, begin to breathe more deeply—longer inhalations and longer exhalations. With deep breathing, you breathe from your diaphragm, from your gut. Notice the three parts to your breathing—your chest rises, your ribs expand, and your belly rises as you breathe in. Place your hands on your chest for several breaths, then your ribs, and finally your belly, to feel the breath moving through you. Breathe deeply and slowly, focusing all of your attention on each breath. Don't rush it or breathe quickly. As you exhale naturally, allow any tension to leave you with the breath. Imagine the tension draining from your body and mind as you exhale.

Erotic Massage

Erotic massage is a great way for partners to warm up to each other and reach climax. With the proper setting, the right lubrication, and diverse types of rubbing and stimulation, massage can bring a whole new erotic dimension to your lovemaking.

Oil or lotion is a must-have in erotic massage. If you're stimulating your man, use oil-based or water-based lubricants. If you're stimulating your woman, only use water-based lubricants to avoid vaginal infection. Letting the lubricant container rest in hot water for a few minutes makes the liquid nice and warm.

Start by rubbing the temples and the shoulders, then the back and the buttocks, followed by the legs and feet, and finally the genitals. If you're massaging your man's lingam, long, slow strokes with an occasional fast and hard thrust will do the job perfectly. If you're bringing a yoni to climax, stimulate the clitoris or G-spot with slow, gentle movements of one hand while rubbing other parts of her body with the other hand. Hot talk is a great addition to the experience.

Scratching

Along with kissing and embracing, Vatsyayana considered scratching an integral part of foreplay. "Nothing tends to increase love so much as the effects of marking with the nails." In fact, men as well as women in ancient India grew one or several nails long specifically for the purpose of scratching their lover.

The *Kama Sutra* offers nearly a dozen tips on scratching techniques; we've boiled them down to just a few. Here goes with the good, the bad, and the ugly.

In many ways scratching isn't all that unusual in the bedroom. Massage, cuddling, and various forms of touch are all used in the bedroom. So, it's not a huge jump to imagine that scratching can also be used to get your partner in the mood.

These scratching techniques are also good to use at various times during the lovemaking process. There are gentle scratches to awaken the sensuality of your partner, and more rough forms of scratching to be used well into the lovemaking process.

- **Scratching Technique #1.** In the first technique, the nails are scraped against the skin of your lover, much like a cat would scratch a tree. These scratches are aggressive, but not necessarily painful. A few areas listed are the lips, the throat, the armpit, and the middle chest.

- **Scratching Technique #2.** The second technique is done extremely gently, so softly, in fact, that it is supposed to raise the hair on your partner's body. A few places recommended are the chin, the forearm, the breasts, the lower lip, and the inner thighs.

- **Scratching Technique #3.** The next technique is done with a slightly rougher scratch. This type of scratch is done in circular movements on the navel, the small cavities about the buttocks, and the joints of the thigh.

- **Scratching Technique #4.** The last technique is done in a rough manner with both hands at once. Here all five nails are used simultaneously across your lover. This technique is used when lover's are fully aroused and already in the act of lovemaking. This technique can then be used on a lover's neck, breasts, buttocks, back, or legs.

Tips for Men on Embracing

There's no better way to beef up your sex life than by executing an arousing embrace with your woman. By doing so, you will warm her to you and get the engines revving. The *Kama Sutra* lays out two basic kinds of embrace you can use to show your interest or to heighten the pleasure.

- **Touching Embrace.** The touching embrace occurs when you stand in front of or alongside a woman and touch your body to hers. Sounds simple, right? It is, but to make anything simple, it takes practice. If you can master this basic form of touch, you will feel confident in your abilities and excite your partner with your direct, intimate style.

- **Pressing Embrace.** The pressing embrace occurs when a man presses a woman up against the wall. Obviously, it's a good idea to know beforehand whether or not your partner wants to be pinned up against a wall, but if you sense she does, then nothing can get her turned on like a little full court press. It shows her you want her and that you want her now. Many women love this kind of take-charge attitude.

Yoni Embraces

Here are some sizzling techniques to better stimulate your partner's sex center:

- **In the Hood.** When first going in for clitoral stimulation, spend some time playing with the hood to loosen her up. Oh so gently push and pull on it, slowly opening it up to expose the clitoris. Once the clitoris is exposed, tease it for a while before applying constant stimulation.

- **Labial Exploration.** With your well-lubricated hand palm down against her vagina, fingers pointing toward the anus, pull up toward her navel to open up her labial folds. With the fingers of your other hand, explore the inner and outer lips with gentle strokes and tugs.

- **Three Finger Thrust.** With two fingers
  inside her vagina, place your thumb against
  her clitoris. Thrusting and twisting your
  fingers slowly as your thumb stimulates her
  clitoris can feel great. Vibrating your entire
  hand is also very hot.

Tips for Women on Embracing

Embracing your man can tell him you're ready to
make love, that you want more of what he's giving
you, or that you're happy he's turned on. It's one
of the best devices you have to encourage him to
dig deeper toward greater sexual satisfaction for
himself and you. The *Kama Sutra* discusses two
basic types of embraces you can use to increase
the intimacy you feel with your man.

- **Piercing Embrace.** The piercing embrace
  takes place when a woman bends down, as
  if to pick something up, and she pierces a
  man with her breasts, who then takes hold
  of them.

- **Rubbing Embrace.** The rubbing embrace
  is one of the simple, yet joyous, pleasures of
  being with a man. There you are, walking
  in a park at dusk, or along the beach after a
  party, and you brush up against each other.
  Such a subtle encounter can send tingles

down your spine and turn the conversation to more sensual topics. By gently rubbing up against a man, you send a clear signal that you're hot for him.

Lingam Embraces

We now describe several different types of lingam embraces. These can be done during the love-making process, or can be done on their own. Remember that each man is different and enjoys different variations on these basic types of embraces and massage techniques.

- **Fire Starter.** Gently rub the penis between two well-oiled hands, as if you were a cave person trying to start a fire by rubbing two sticks together.

- **Head Start.** With one hand holding the penis near the shaft, use the other well-lubed hand to grope and rub the head.

- **Belly Flop.** Rest the penis on the belly. With one hand, cup the balls. With the other, run it up and down the underside of the penis, as if you were petting the belly of a cat.

- **The Old One Two.** One hand goes down from the top to the bottom of the penis, and when it hits the bottom, it lets go. The other hand then repeats the action.

Additional Embraces

The *Kama Sutra* describes a bunch of other embraces that can be used to initiate or enhance sexual activity. By exploring the pleasures of these embraces, a couple can significantly spice up their sex life. The more embraces you know and engage in, the more fun and satisfying you'll find sex!

- **The Twining of a Creeper.** Stand face-to-face, very close together. Wrap your arms and legs around each other. Now, the woman raises one leg and wraps it around the man's thigh. Kiss and caress, or even join in sexual union.

- **Climbing a Tree.** In this expansion of the twining of a creeper embrace, stand close with your arms around each other (see Figure 4.1). Now, the woman places one foot on the man's foot and wraps the other leg around his thigh like she's trying to climb him. This embrace is hottest when the woman uses this climbing motion to reach up to kiss her man.

- **Mixing Sesame Seed with Rice Embrace.** Lie very close together. Let the man place his leg between the woman's thighs and then she wraps herself around him (see Figure 4.2). The overlapping and intertwining of the bodies makes it hard to tell one from the other, and the resulting intimacy is deeply satisfying.

Figure 4.1 *Climbing the Tree.*

Figure 4.2   *Mixing Sesame Seed with Rice.*

> ### Kama Sutra Words
>
> The *Kama Sutra* refers to **jaghana**, which is the area between the navel and the thighs on both male and female bodies.

- **Milk and Water Embrace.** The man sits on the edge of the bed and the woman straddles his lap, facing him. Then, embrace each other tightly, drawing your bodies into maximum intimacy. This is a great position to get the passion churning.

- **Embrace of the Thighs.** Each partner uses his or her thighs to grip the other's thighs. This pulls your bodies close together and positions the penis against the front of the woman. This position works lying down, sitting, or standing.

- **Embrace of the *Jaghana*.** In this embrace, the man presses his jaghana against the woman's. Simulating intercourse in this position can be very arousing. Penetration never occurs, but it is hinted at and the necessary energies are brought forth.

- **Embrace of the Breasts.** Stand or sit close together, and let the man press his chest against the woman's breast as she presses in return. Arching your heads back and looking into each other's eyes makes this a great way to exchange loving signals and to increase the intimacy and passion.

- **Embrace of the Forehead.** Sit or stand facing each other. One partner kisses, caresses, or brushes against the other's forehead. Likewise, try placing your foreheads together and looking into each other's eyes. As your spirits mix, your passion will rise.

Sexy Play

No discussion of embracing would be complete without exploring some of the many sex toy options available. These toys can enhance any sexual experience, especially during the embrace phase of sexual play.

Here's a breakdown of some of the most popular ones and a few ideas on how to use them most effectively:

- **Dildo.** A lingam-shaped object, usually made of acrylic, rubber, or glass. It can be used to penetrate the yoni during cunnilingus or the anus during lingam-to-yoni intercourse. Some dildos (and vibrators)

continues

continued

come with multiple shafts and heads for stimulating various areas at once.

- **Vibrator.** A lingam-shaped object that vibrates through battery-power. Vibrators, like dildos, come in all shapes and sizes, and some even strap on so a woman can simulate lingam thrusting. The vibrations bring extra pleasure.

- **Vibrating erection rings.** These devices fit snuggly around the shaft of the penis, trapping the blood at the tip, which can increase pleasure. The attached "vibrating bullet" stimulates the clitoris during intercourse and increases pleasure for the woman.

- **Beads and balls.** By inserting a row of beads or small balls into the yoni or anus, pleasure can be had by slowly removing them. With each "pop," arousal increases.

The Least You Need to Know

- There are many forms of passion, ranging in levels of intensity and excitement.

- Having various sexual and nonsexual forms of touch in your life creates lasting passion and happiness.

- Gazing into your partner's eyes can lead to deep intimacy and trust.

- An unorthodox method of caressing is to experiment with lightly scratching your partner using your nails.

Chapter 5

Kissing

In This Chapter

- Unusual places to kiss your lover
- Types of kissing
- Keeping your lips soft
- "Functional" kisses

We all remember our first kiss. For most of us, it was our entry into sexuality. It brought to our lips the taste of another's eager flesh, and we emerged from the experience dizzy, aroused, and totally hooked.

The kiss is recognized the world over as the sign of intimacy. By kissing someone with an open mouth you send a strong message of sensual interest. Whether we kiss to share our vital breath, or to simply get nice and hot, one thing's for certain—kissing gets the juices flowing.

The *Kama Sutra* has a lot to say about how to use kissing most effectively to improve sexual activity. By using a diversity of kisses, you will more deeply stimulate and evoke the unknown passions of your lover. And for creating intimacy, nothing beats a nice long wet kiss. So kiss often, kiss deeply, and kiss in many ways, because there's no better way to say, "I want you."

Sexy Play

Men need to consider their facial hair before heading into a heavy kissing session. If you have a beard, then you should keep it trim and conditioned. Trimming it takes off the sharp, pointy ends, and treating it regularly with hair conditioner keeps it soft.

If you don't have a beard, then there's nothing crueler than making your woman kiss you with a day of stubble. It's like asking her to kiss sandpaper. Women appreciate few gestures more than a smooth, freshly shaven face, and it's the best way to encourage her to let you put it wherever you want.

Places to Kiss

The sky's the limit when it comes to kissable spots on your lover. Most people restrict themselves to just a few locales—the mouth, the breasts, the

neck—but erotic experts range over their lovers'
bodies like an explorer over the globe, leaving no
stone unturned, no mountain unclimbed. By kissing
new and different regions of your partner's body,
you will open your partner to new passions and
improve the overall sexual experience for you both.

Sexy Play

The softest place is always the most
kissable. Follow these preparation tips
for hours of hot kissing.

- **Soft lips.** Nothing turns your lover off
  like dry, cracked lips. On the other
  hand, supple, soft lips are a major
  turn-on. To keep them nice and soft
  apply lip gloss or ointment several
  times a day and exfoliate your lips
  with a soft brush once a week.

- **Soft facial skin.** For both the ladies
  and the men, keeping your facial
  skin soft is a good idea as well.
  Basic lotion or cream will do the job.
  Smooth faces glide more easily over
  one another, and they're more satisfying to kiss and gentler on the Lips.

Kissing is not only for the lips. What follows is
a list of several unusual places you can kiss your
lover.

- **Forehead.** Believe it or not, the forehead is a surprisingly sensitive area. By kissing your lover's forehead, brushing your lips lightly across his brow, you give a message of both passion and respect. In a sense, you are kissing the shell of his mind, sending desire signals directly into his innermost thoughts.

- **Eyes.** As the eyes of your lover close to relish the ecstasy of your touch, try a few gentle kisses on the eyelids. First one, then the other, and then back to the first. The precious nature of the eyes makes eye kissing particularly sensuous, and due to the eyes' close relation to the brain, a kiss on the lids can excite your lover's entire body.

- **Cheeks.** Mothers call their babies' cheeks "kissing pads," and the same could be said of your lover's cheeks. Those soft facial pillows are perfect landing pads for zealous lips. Whether it's a light peck or a series of deep, sloppy sucks, spending some time with your lover's cheeks is always a great arousal device.

- **Throat.** When predatory animals meet in the wild, they bear their throats to one another to show they come in peace. By kissing, sucking, or nibbling gently on your lover's neck, you show him that you also come in peace. And as most of us know, the nerve channels that reach down the spine make having your throat and neck kissed a highly arousing experience. Let the hickies begin!

Tidbits of Pleasure

If there's one message the *Kama Sutra* has about sex, it's that it should be fun. Here's a playful kissing game it recommends. Just be careful not to bite too hard!

With regards to kissing, a wager may be laid as to which will get hold of the lips of the other first. If the woman loses, she should pretend to cry, should keep her lover off by shaking her hands, and turn away from him and dispute with him saying, "Let another wager be laid."

If she loses this a second time, she should appear doubly distressed, and when her lover is off his guard or asleep, she should get hold of his lower lip, and hold it in her teeth, so that it should not slip away. Then she should laugh, make a loud noise, deride him, dance about, and say whatever she likes in a joking way, moving her eyebrows and rolling her eyes.

Such are the wagers and quarrels as far as kissing is concerned. All these, however, are only peculiar to men and women of intense passion.

Types of Kissing

The *Kama Sutra* describes various types of kissing, each perfectly designed to excite you and your partner in different ways. Using a variety of kisses in one lovemaking session is the best way to extend arousal and spice things up. Few things are more satisfying than making out with someone who switches up his kissing styles!

- **Nominal kiss.** Here, only the lips touch. An introduction is made, gently and curiously. The lovers test each other's taste and interest, and linger awhile in each other's growing responsiveness.

- **Throbbing kiss.** Moving from the nominal kiss, your lips against your lover's, and in return, your lover moves his lower lip. The "throbbing" element comes from the surge in passion and the quivering of the lips. While the lovers are still only touching mouths, this kiss indicates a desire for more.

- **Touching kiss.** Like a cobra rising from its nest, extend your tongue extend outward to gently touch your lover's lip. Then, both of you reach out with your hands and begin holding and caressing each other. Drawing closer, your passion mounts.

- **Straight kiss.** The straight kiss is like the nominal kiss, only the lovers come in "straight" at each other, tilting their heads only enough to move their noses aside and meet lips. This head position keeps things fairly tame, though touching and caressing may also be occurring. The Straight Kiss is a great way to show initial affection and even a slight arousing shyness.

- **Bent kiss.** This kiss is the full-on deal, bringing the lips into a deep, locked position and allowing for maximum tongue penetration. The lovers also caress each other with abandon. For ultimate closeness, one lover might place his hand behind the other's neck and pull inward.

- **Turned kiss.** A great, but gentle, take-charge technique, this kiss occurs when one partner takes his lover's face in his hands and turns it upward. Then, slowly and sensuously, the kiss is delivered. With the face turned in this fashion, lips and tongues interlock deeply and passionately.

- **Pressed kiss.** As the name suggests, this kiss involves pressure. One lover presses firmly against the other's lower lip with a lip or finger. This can also involve one lover holding the other's lower lip and then gently touching it with his tongue, ending in a fuller lip kiss. The Pressed Kiss is a sure sign of desire for deeper contact.

- **Kiss of the upper lip.** This kiss takes place when one lover kisses or sucks the upper lip of their lover while the other kisses or sucks on their lower lip. The upper lip is extremely sensitive, especially on the inside. By switching who's on top and who's on bottom, this is a love game that could arouse for hours.

- **Clasping kiss.** Here, one lover takes the other's lips firmly into his own. The clasp that results mimics sexual union and brings forth arousal. When the tongues enter the action, this results in the next kind of kiss.

- **Wrestling of tongues.** In what is commonly known as tonguing or French kissing, this kiss involves full tongue action. The tongue can be used to touch or lick your lover's lips, teeth, gums, or tongue. And the tongue play can be slow and light, fast and furious, and even somewhat combative (the *Kama Sutra* even calls it "fighting of the tongues"). Nothing transmits the urgent message of your desires like a probing, hungry tongue.

The Four Methods of Kissing

The *Kama Sutra* states that there are four methods of kisses, depending on the part of the body being kissed:

- **Soft kiss.** A soft kiss is for the breasts and the areas where the limbs join the body. Gentle nips and tongue teasing do the trick.

- **Moderate kiss.** A moderate kiss is for the cheeks, breasts, belly, and hips. Due to the extra flesh in these areas, gentle nibbles with the teeth are recommended as well.

- **Full-on kiss.** A full-on moves around your lover's body, using the tongue to follow the curves, travel around the breasts, and linger at the bellybutton.

- **Contracted kiss.** A contracted kiss happens when you start by gently drawing your nails over your lover's body, and then kiss them passionately on the lips at the same time.

Functional Kisses

Kisses can be used to meet different ends, with different intentions, and in a variety of love games. By kissing your lover, you send a message, you make a request, you assert a position. In other words, your kisses are love tools that you can use to steer each erotic session in the right direction.

- **Kiss that kindles love.** When a woman looks into the face of her lover as he sleeps, and then kisses it to awaken him for erotic play, this is called "a kiss that kindles love."

It shows the admiration a woman feels for the body of her sleeping lover, and it's a great way to start the day. Starting off with gentle kisses that barely register and then moving onto more passionate kisses will send subtle love messages into your lover's dreams and waken him primed and ready to go.

- **Kiss that turns away.** Sometimes a man needs to be reminded of the good things in life. Maybe he's engaged in business, looking at something (or someone!) else, or maybe you two are fighting. By giving him a kiss, in front or from behind, you "turn him away" from these distractions and "turn him on" to better things.

- **Kiss that awakens.** Men can also awaken their lover with a kiss. This happens when he returns home late and she is still asleep. Kissing her, he awakens her to his desire for lovemaking. The *Kama Sutra* even suggests that women fake being asleep in order to "know his intention and obtain respect from him." Today we call this "playing hard to get."

- **Kiss that shows intention.** It might sound a little corny, but this technique can really turn someone on. Next time you see an image of your lover in the mirror or in the water, turn and kiss it. This "kiss that shows intention" is truly a romantic way to show someone you haven't kissed yet that you'd like to.

- **Transferred kiss.** Similar to the previous kiss, this involves kissing a picture, object, or person that is dear to your lover in your lover's presence. The kiss is thereby "transferred" to your lover. With the right look of suggestion, such a move can generate quick requests for the real thing.

- **Demonstrative kiss.** This is a kiss used to send a message of interested affection. A man walks up to a woman in public and kisses her hand.

The Least You Need to Know

- Kissing is good anytime—before, during, or after sex.

- Keeping your lips and skin silky soft is important.

- Remember, you can kiss your partner anywhere on his body.

- Kissing techniques tend to be subtle, meaning that focusing on the small details when kissing will make the experience more pleasurable.

Chapter 6

Lingam and Yoni Kisses

In This Chapter

- Oral sex techniques to pleasure a man
- Oral sex techniques to pleasure a woman
- Oral sex variations for men
- Oral sex variations for women

Now known as *fellatio* and *cunnilingus*, the lingam and yoni kisses have been around since men and women have been pleasuring each other. For women, receiving cunnilingus is a wonderful way to reach climax, as it allows for direct clitoral stimulation using the lips and tongue. For men, receiving fellatio is a sensuous alternative to coitus, as the dexterity of the mouth, lips, and tongue provide for a variety of stimulation techniques.

As natural as pleasuring your partner with your mouth can sometimes seem, these sex practices are actually quite complex and full of exciting challenges and opportunities. By learning how to better please your lover orally, you not only open up a whole new horizon of sensual sharing, but you are more likely to receive great oral pleasure in return. In this chapter, we tell you all you need to know to help your chosen one reach climax through outstanding oral stimulation.

The Eight Lingam Kisses

These days, fellatio is the art of sucking or licking or on the penis with one's mouth. The vast majority of men find fellatio extremely stimulating and satisfying, and it is a wonderful intimate way for two lovers to bond.

> ### *Kama Sutra* Words
>
> **Fellatio** comes from the Latin verb, *fellare*, which means "to suck." **Cunnilingus** comes from Latin word *connus* which combines both "vulva" and "lingere" which means to lick.

The *Kama Sutra* lists eight types of lingam kisses. Mixing these up makes for an ideal experience for a man. When it comes to bringing your man to climax with your mouth, it's always best to use a variety of techniques, from slow and gentle to fast and hard, culminating in the grand prize of climax.

Lingam kisses can be performed in an array of positions. With the man standing, lying down, sitting, or hovering over his partner. And the giver of fellatio can kneel, lie down, stand up and bend over, or whatever gets the mouth in motion. Trying different positions during one session is also a good idea.

 Sexy Play

Getting him ready for lingam kisses:

- Lingam kisses can be a great way to get your man in the mood. For women, try kneeling on the floor, looking him in the eyes, and sucking on your finger for a while. This will arouse him to no end and prepare him for the real thing.

- Blowing on his penis with your hot breath will also cause him major excitement.

- One warning, no teeth. The teeth can never touch the lingam. Period. You need to use your lips and tongue. Any contact with teeth—even one tooth—is distracting and may be painful.

For the men, remember to let your partner know what feels good and only have an orgasm in her mouth if she wants you to.

For the women, we recommend you start by using your hands and mouth to stimulate his thighs, belly, and scrotum. Then moving to his testicles and shaft. Also, make sure your lips are wet and use a lot of saliva for lubrication.

Also, if you don't want him to have an orgasm in your mouth, remove his lingam and let him climax elsewhere.

The following are the lingam kisses identified in the *Kama Sutra*:

- **Nominal Congress.** Gripping our partner's lingam, take it slowly into your mouth and move it around in there. Pressing your lips against it to create a gentle sucking action, slowly pull your mouth away.

- **Side Nibbling.** This lingam kiss is best done with the man standing up and the woman kneeling in front of him (see Figure 6.). Hold the tip of the lingam with your fingers. Lick up and down the side of the lingam, occasionally kissing and caressing it. Switch off between hard and soft hand and lip pressure.

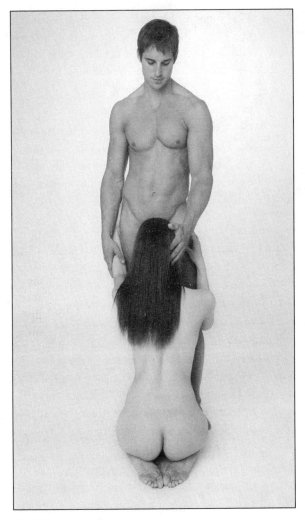

Figure 6.1 *Lingam kiss standing.*

- **Pressing the Outside.** With closed lips, press against the head of the lingam, kissing it. Then suck lightly on the lingam, as if you were trying to suck something out of it.

- **Pressing the Inside.** This type of lingam kiss is sure to bring the man to orgasm.

  Bring the lingam fully into your mouth with your lips pressed tight around it. Suck on the lingam and draw it out of your mouth. Repeat this arousing gesture and climax will soon follow.

Sexy Play

For variety, you can perform lingam kisses while having an ice cube or mint in your mouth. The man is sure to react.

- **Kissing.** Holding the lingam with your hand around the base, kiss the tip and shaft in the same way you would kiss his mouth. Any kind of kiss will do in this situation—light tender kisses, wet sloppy kisses, and everything in between.

- **Rubbing.** This actually refers to stimulating the lingam with your tongue. Run your tongue up and down the lingam and then jostle it around the lingam head. Using the tip of your tongue as well as the fat, main part brings extra pleasure.

- **Sucking a Mango Fruit.** Bringing the lingam halfway into your mouth, you suck on it with intense pressure. Simulate the way you would suck on a mango or a lollipop. Varying this with gentle, more open-mouth sucks is highly arousing to a man.

- **Swallowing Up.** This type of lingam kiss is best done when the man is laying down and the woman is laying between his legs (see Figure 6.2).

  Swallowing up is otherwise known as "deep throating," this involves bringing the lingam as far into your throat as possible. Making throat movements like you are swallowing the lingam brings extra stimulation to the tip and is very pleasurable for the man. If you have a strong gag reflex you may not want to experiment with this position.

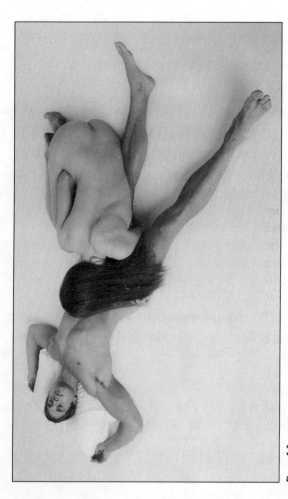

Figure 6.2 *Lingam kiss lying down.*

The Seven Yoni Kisses

Cunnilingus is the art of pleasing a woman by licking and sucking the various parts of her vaginal area—the clitoris, the labia, and the vaginal opening or vestibule. Most women find this to be a highly pleasurable experience and anyone seeking to keep a woman's long-term interest in sex is best to learn the art of cunnilingus.

For many women, cunnilingus is the best way to achieve orgasm. Because of the direct and continual clitoral stimulation that cunnilingus provides, it is often a better way for a woman to reach climax than intercourse. Just like the flexibility of the mouth is highly pleasing to the penis, so can the lips and tongue provide a more diverse, and therefore, satisfying experience for the yoni.

Yoni kissing can be done in a variety of positions. The woman can lie down on her back or stomach on a bed and make her yoni available to her partner's mouth. She can also stand against a wall with one leg on a chair or around her partner's neck. Finally, with her partner lying on his back, she can squat over his face and place her yoni in direct contact with his mouth. If she then brings her mouth to his lingam, this state of "69" can bring both partners to a mutual climax.

A good way to start cunnilingus is for the man to spend an extra long time kissing, licking, and nibbling her inner thighs, while slowly moving up to her yoni.

From there, the man can start licking the upper tip of the clitoris, just under the hood. From there he can suck her yoni while gently rubbing her labia.

Sexy Play

Enhancing cunnilingus:

- Some people report that using flavored oils on your partner's vulva while doing these exercises can be a fun addition.

- Many women go crazy for the combination of sex toys with oral sex.

- Some women report that their favorite position for oral sex is to have their legs spread open with their partner kneeling in front of them.

- Remember that the clitoris is extremely sensitive and if you over stimulate the clit, it can hurt. This means if you rub too fast, too long, or too hard it can be painful.

The following are the yoni kisses described in the *Kama Sutra*:

- **Pressing Yoni Kiss.** Pretending that the yoni is a mouth, press your lips against it, giving it a gentle kiss. With your tongue remaining in your mouth, repeat this act of respect several times. With your hands, stimulate the surrounding areas—legs, belly, and breasts.

- **Outer Yoni Tongue Strokes.** In this yoni kiss, you begin to go deeper. With your fingers, open your partner's yoni lips gently and slowly. With your tongue and lips, begin to probe the inner recesses of her lotus flower.

- **Inner Yoni Tongue Strokes.** This form of yoni kiss is to be done with the woman standing up and the man kneeling before her, kissing her yoni (see Figure 6.3).

  The labia are made up of inner and outer lips. In this stroke, open the outer labia and lick and kiss the inner lips with your tongue and lips.

- **Kissing the Yoni Blossom.** Opening her labia with your fingers, you expose her clitoris. With your tongue, run up each side of her labia, ending at the clitoris. Long, sensual licks and sucks up and down her yoni will bring her intense pleasure.

- **Flutter of the Butterfly.** After a few kisses to the yoni, flutter your tongue over her clitoris. You want your tongue to be stiff and for her to feel like butterfly wings are brushing up against her clitoral shaft.

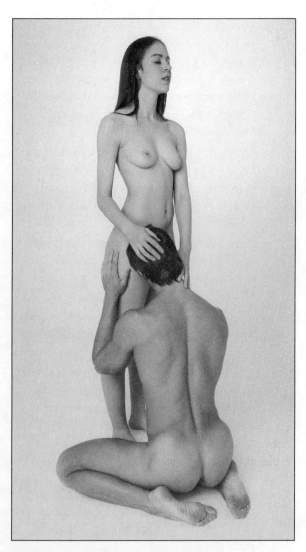

Figure 6.3 *Kiss of the Penetrating Tongues.*

- **Sucking the Yoni Blossom.** Put your lips over the clitoris and gently suck inward. Rub it periodically with your tongue. As you suck on the clitoris, pull out gently with your mouth as if you are sucking an oyster from its shell.

- **Kiss of the Penetrating Tongues.** This type of yoni kiss is best done with the woman lying down in bed with her legs spread open (see Figure 6.4).

  Once your partner's yoni grows flush with blood as her arousal heightens, gently thrust your tongue in and out of her vaginal opening. Once you've loosened her up a bit, plunge your tongue in as far as it will go and lick the inner walls of her vestibule.

- **Drinking from the Fountain of Life.** Your partner's yoni will exude sexual fluids as you lick and kiss it. Enjoy these liquids. They are considered holy and energizing.

- **Kiss of the Crow.** Otherwise known as "sixty-nine," the Kiss of the Crow is a wonderful way for partners to share genital kissing and reach mutual climax. It can be done with the partners lying side by side, or one partner can lie down and the other get on top (see Figure 6.5). The best way to make the Kiss of the Crow a successful sexual experience is to take it slowly, to let one partner give and one partner receive, and to eventually arrive at mutual stimulation for the final phase culminating in climax.

Figure 6.4 *Kiss of the Penetrating Tongues.*

Figure 6.5   *Kiss of the Crow.*

The Least You Need to Know

- When performing yoni kisses or lingam kisses be sensitive to your partner's level of vulnerability.
- Oral sex tends to easily push both men and women to orgasm.
- For women, be very gentle with when kissing the lingam; any teeth involved can cause great pain.
- For men, remember that the clitoris is extremely sensitive and if you overstimulate the clit it can hurt.

Chapter 7

Basic Unions

In This Chapter

- The three different types of timing during sex
- Basic unions
- The work of a man
- The work of a woman

There's more to sexual union than the old "in-and-out." The congress of the lingam and the yoni carries with it a wide variety of sensual options. By learning the many ways of making love, and mixing these ways up in a single love session, lovers can achieve a far more pleasurable erotic experience.

The *Kama Sutra* splits up its wisdom on "basic *unions*" into three kinds: things for men to do, things for women to do, and types of unions (otherwise known as "sexual positions"). In this taxonomy lies the secret to great sex: Both the man *and* the woman need to be proactive about stimulating and being stimulated, and one great way to do this is through different sexual positions. If both lovers embrace their role in enhancing the love game, the sky is the limit!

> **Kama Sutra Words** _____
>
> The *Kama Sutra* uses **union** to refer to sexual position. The word union refers to a man and woman joining as one sexually, spiritually, and emotionally.

The trick in sexuality is to communicate. A lot of time can be saved if you both communicate what you like and what you don't like. Oftentimes, all it takes is a little guidance: "harder, lighter, no teeth, more teeth," and so on. If you can't find the words, in the heat of passion, try to communicate through carefully communicated moans and groans to encourage your partner.

The Three Types of Timing

Before learning the basic unions, we need to look at the different types of timing during the lovemaking process.

According to the *Kama Sutra* the three types of timing are: short, moderate, and long. A match between a man and a woman with equal timing sense is the most likely to produce the highest quality sex. A man who likes his love sessions to go on forever is best matched with a woman of the same sensibility. And a woman who likes it fast and hard is going to be most satisfied with a man who prefers the same.

Timing is an important, challenging, and often overlooked element in sexual relations. Talking about timing with your partner, and working with him or her to achieve the right mix of short, moderate, and long lovemaking sessions, is the best way to maintain a sexual relationship full of flow and satisfaction.

The Work of the Man

In this section, we look at a variety of thrusting techniques a man can use to satisfy himself and his partner. Most of these techniques can be used in any position, as long as the lingam has the necessary access to the yoni.

The *Kama Sutra* is clear to make sure men know their role in sexuality. It's a man's responsibility to use his lingam in diverse ways to please himself and his partner. By utilizing the following advice, "the work of the man," always part of his pleasure, can also become "the pleasure of the woman."

Moving Forward

The moving forward position is perhaps the simplest position mentioned in the *Kama Sutra*. The man places his lingam in the yoni. He then moves his lingam straight in and out. Varying the pace and power of the thrust can heighten the pleasure for both lovers.

Despite the *Kama Sutra's* emphasis on diverse sex positions, it also recognizes the beauty in simple moves, and the moving forward position is the simplest. Using this thrust at various times during your lovemaking session, but not all the time, is a great way to keep the pleasure going.

Churning

The man holds his lingam in his hand and swirls it around inside his partner's yoni. In essence, the man is making like he's churning butter. This can be very satisfying to the woman as the man probes and stimulates various undertouched parts of her yoni, and it can also be satisfying for the man to use his lingam in this assertive manner. Be careful, however, not to churn too wide, or you could cause pain.

This move, along with striking, is a small example of the fun that can be had when the man takes his lingam into his hand and touches the woman with it. Holding his lingam, he can rub it against her breasts or nipples, along the rim of her buttocks, across her mouth, or anywhere else that seems arousing. The woman should relax and enjoy this phallic play, knowing that it gives the man con-fidence and entices him to further penetration.

Piercing

The woman lies down on her back so that her yoni is low down. The man then enters her with his lingam in such a way that each thrust strokes her clitoris.

Piercing is a great position because it enables both partners to feel deep sexual arousal during inter-course. The man's shaft rubbing against her clitoris will make it easier for her to climax during penetration. Other ways to stimulate the clitoris during penetration include the man using his fingers, a vibrator, or the woman stimulating herself.

Rubbing

There are two ways to make this position work. Either the woman lies on her back with a pillow under her buttocks and he mounts her in missionary position or the woman lies with her yoni open at the edge of the bed and the man stands or kneels at the edge.

The man then penetrates the woman and moves in such a way that his thrusting lingam rubs against the bottom of her vagina and her perineum. The pressure downward on the base of her yoni will bring her increased pleasure.

Pressing

The man thrusts his lingam into the woman's yoni as far as it will go. He then holds it there at its greatest depth until each lover experiences the height of pleasure from this position. Pulling out, he repeats the thrust.

By pushing his lingam as far in as it can go, the man is stimulating the innermost parts of the yoni. As his pelvis presses up against the outer labia and clitoral hood, both partners will feel a contact buzz from prolonged pressure. Finally, the vaginal walls will begin to contract and emit intense pleasure signals to the woman.

Striking

The man takes his lingam in his hand and gently slaps the woman's yoni. All parts of the yoni should enjoy this action, but especially the clitoris. The tapping or slapping can vary from very light to heavy, but the man should be careful not to hurt the woman or seem overly aggressive.

The idea behind the thrill of striking is simple: Constant stimulation is nice, but it's also nice when one stimulates in an on-again-off-again manner. Striking is pleasurable because there's a break. The lingam taps the yoni, and then there's a pause, followed by another strike. The "tease and conquer" element in this move is highly arousing to most women.

The Blow of the Boar

The man places his lingam in the woman's yoni. Angling his body, he begins to thrust in and out, putting pressure on one side of the vagina. Once he's worked one side, he moves to the other.

Many men forget that the yoni is a "many sided organ." By stimulating one side only, the man not only provides pleasure on that side, but he gives a rest to the other side, which makes stimulating that side even more pleasurable because there's been a break in the action. The man who impresses his woman with attention to the "many sides" of her yoni is certain to be a highly coveted lover.

The Blow of the Bull

The man penetrates the yoni with his lingam and attempts during thrusting to rub both sides of the vaginal vestibule. Making a swirling motion as he thrusts can make for maximum two-sided contact. The man should concentrate on "filling" the vagina and working it from all angles.

When a man is engaged in a thrust move like the blow of the bull, he should not forget to maintain eye contact, at least occasionally, with the woman. This thrust can be either very personal or very impersonal. Of course, there's nothing wrong with either, but there's something special about both. Women usually prefer a sense of intimacy to accompany their lovemaking, so be the Bull, but also let her know it's you.

The Sporting of the Sparrow

In this thrust, the man moves his lingam up and down inside his partner's yoni at an increasing speed. Working together, the partners move in sync and head together toward that irresistible and mutual moment of release.

From the Master

"Though a woman is reserved, and keeps her feelings concealed; yet when she gets on the top of a man, she then shows all her love and desire."

Orgasm for a man usually comes after continuous and steady stimulation of his lingam. The sporting of the sparrow is an excellent way to make this happen. Women will also find this thrust to be pleasurable. Many women enjoy the feeling of "pounding" that accompanies this thrust. And joined with direct clitoral stimulation, it's a win-win situation for both lovers.

The Work of the Woman

Despite some stereotypes about men being the "active" ones in intercourse, there's a wide variety of actions a woman can take to initiate, alter, and improve sexual union. It's important that the man make room for the woman to take the initiative and control the lovemaking now and then.

The three positions described here are "woman on top" positions. Nevertheless, even if a woman is "on bottom," she has ample opportunity to move her body in various ways to enhance the sexual union. In all cases, the man should be receptive to the signals a woman is sending him about what she wants and where she wants the lovemaking to go.

The Pair of Tongs

The man should lie on his back. The woman then faces him and straddles his lingam with her knees bent (see Figure 7.1). She then presses his lingam with her vaginal muscles, constricting the blood in both for heightened pleasure.

When in this position, there's ample room for both partners to enjoy each other in a variety of ways. Each can use his or her hands to stimulate and caress the other's body. From this position, gyrating movements in the pelvis can bring profound arousal. The penetration achieved is also very deep and brings the lovers to the edge of new pleasure boundaries.

Figure 7.1 *The Pair of Tongs.*

The Top

The Top is a great position that includes three different sections. The position starts with the man on his back. The woman faces and straddles him (see Figure 7.2). At the same time she raises her legs up so that only her feet are on the bed and the rest of her body is on top of him (see Figure 7.3).

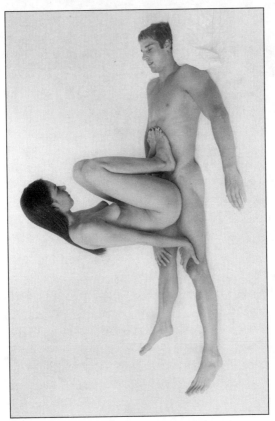

Figure 7.2   *The Top, starting position.*

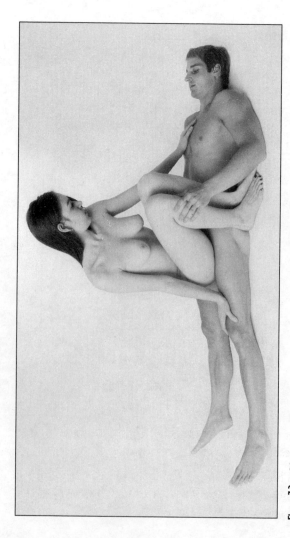

Figure 7.3 *She raises her legs.*

Tidbits of Pleasure

We all know that one sexual partner often gets tired before another. What to do? Arouse your lover back into action!

The *Kama Sutra* has a specific recommendation for women, probably because men tend to tire out before them, but the same tactics can work for the guys. "When a woman sees that her lover is fatigued by constant congress, without having his desire satisfied, she should, with his permission, lay him down upon his back, and give him assistance by acting his part. She may also do this to satisfy the curiosity of her lover, or her own desire of novelty."

Next, using her hands for balance, she then swivels around until her back is to his face (see Figure 7.4). In this position she can intensify the experience by rubbing his chest. She can also alter her angle for variety. During the last part of the Top she continues the spinning motion until she's turned fully around to the original position and is facing him (see Figure 7.5).

The *Kama Sutra* is careful to point out that this move takes a lot of practice, but, hey, there are worse things you could be doing!

Figure 7.4 *She swivels around.*

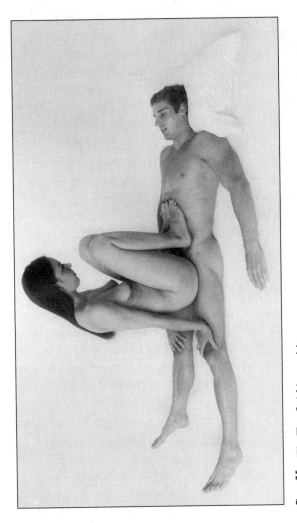

Figure 7.5   *The Top, finishing position.*

The Swing

This is a position made possible by stopping half way through the top position. Once the woman has swiveled around and her back is to her lover's face, she then sits up and bends over and puts her hands on his legs (see Figure 7.6). From this position, she can gently swing and thrust her yoni on his lingam.

If the man is strong enough, he can push his abdomen upward, thrusting his lingam in a "moving forward" way. He can also stroke and squeeze her buttocks and kiss and caress her back and neck. The angle of the lingam in the yoni in this position should be highly enticing for both partners.

The Mare's Position

This is a variant of the swing. Instead of leaning forward, the woman leans back into the man. He is leaning back on his arms to hold her up (see Figure 7.7). Then, using her vaginal muscles, she "clasps" on the man's lingam, holding him in her. This direct pressure is intensely arousing to the lingam and empowering for the woman.

From this position, the man can reach around and stimulate the woman's breasts and nipples. The couple can also touch cheeks and communicate verbally at an intimate level. Finally, the man can reach around and caress the inner thighs of the woman, increasing her state of arousal.

Figure 7.6 *The Swing.*

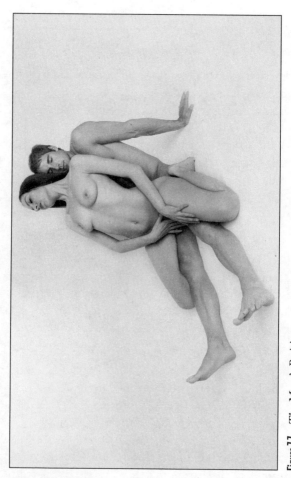

Figure 7.7 *The Mare's Position.*

Kinds of Unions

Once you've mastered the thrusts and positions described above, you should move on to enjoying the more complex positions in this section. All of these positions involve sitting upright, and most of them involve placing the lingam in the yoni. With their potential for eye-to-eye contact and deep penetration, they're an arousing alternative to the lying down positions.

Entwined Lotus Union

Both partners sit in something like the lotus position, but their legs are wrapped around each other—hence the name, "entwined lotus." They then place their arms around each other's necks in an embrace. Staring closely into each other's eyes, they move together in a coordinated state of excitement. Kissing and caressing, they stimulate each other through sight and touch.

The lotus position has been used for centuries to help people achieve inner peace and enlightenment during meditation. By keeping the back straight and letting your energy run directly up the spine, the lotus position opens up your sex centers to ultimate flow. By sharing touch and sexual intimacy in this entwining embrace, lovers can bond both physically and spiritually, increasing their pleasure.

Union of Hands and Feet

The man begins by sitting knees apart and feet almost together. The woman then straddles him with her knees bent and her feet to the side of his buttocks. Guiding the lingam into the yoni, the couple deeply unites. Then, by grabbing each other's feet, the lovers create a circle of energy that increases their passion.

This position highlights the importance of energy flow during lovemaking. Many of us simply think of the lingam and yoni as being the places where "sex happens." However, don't forget that lovers' bodies are intertwining into a circuit of passion, and by touching each other in various ways, these circuits open up for greater enjoyment. Especially important in this regard are the hands—don't just let your hands sit there during lovemaking, but use them to stimulate your partner and create "circles of contact" that enhance energy flow.

Compact Union

In the compact union the woman is lying on her back but her legs are drawn upward either toward or against her body. The result is that her yoni is spread wider and deeper lingam penetration is possible. This type of union can expose her clitoris to more frequent and direct stimulation.

The man, often propped up on his knees, then penetrates her. By grasping her thighs, he can gain greater control over his thrusts. By leaning in, he can stimulate the woman's breasts with his mouth. The deep penetration made possible by the wide-open yoni adds to the excitement of the clitoral stimulation.

Acquiring Union

Sitting with his legs slightly spread, the man takes the woman onto is lap, placing his lingam in her yoni. The woman lifts her knees to his elbows and hugs the man with her legs. The man then pulls her closer to him by hugging her shoulders or neck, and the two rock back and forth in a state of ecstatic union (see Figure 7.8).

This is an extremely intimate position, and one in which mutual orgasm can often be achieved, especially when the man and woman take special care to move together. This is also a great position for quiet sex talk and love whispers. More than anything, this position provides for a degree of closeness.

Figure 7.8 *Acquiring Union.*

Union Like a Tortoise

The man sits in the lotus position. The woman sits in his lap facing him. With the lingam in the yoni, the couple then joins matching parts—hands to hands, arms to arms, chest to chest, eye to eye, and mouth to mouth. United in utter intimacy, their sensual energies flow freely and deeply.

The goal here is to align the matching parts. By aligning them, the energy flows more freely between the partners. Try to notice the tingling sensations in your aligned body parts, and concentrate on sending warm and stimulating energies toward your lover. The resulting "energy field" will greatly heighten intimacy and arousal.

Union of Full Enclosure

This position begins in the union like a tortoise. The man then places his arms under the woman's legs, hoisting them upward and opening her yoni for deeper penetration and fuller contact with her clitoris. The resulting passion is intense and mutually pleasurable.

If the man is strong enough in his arms, he can hoist the woman up and down on his lingam. The pressure on the thighs should open the yoni to new proportions, increasing the pleasure for the woman. Kissing and pecking each other during this position adds an extra thrill.

Union of Ecstatic Delight

Sitting on his heels with his knees bent, the man guides the yoni of the straddling woman onto his lingam. With his hands in the small of her back, he holds her suspended and moves her around on his lingam as she leans back on her hands. As for how this feels, the name says it all.

This position requires arm and leg strength in the man and abdominal and leg strength in the woman, and if the strength is there, pleasure will be had. The pubic bone of the woman will appear prominently in this position, so it's a good opportunity for the man to stroke it with one of his hands. This is also a great position for the woman to use her entire body to do some power thrusting.

The Least You Need to Know

- During lovemaking there are three types of timing: short, moderate, and long.
- For best results in the bedroom, it's important to try to match your lover's timing.

- As the *Kama Sutra* states, the secret to great sex is for both the man and the woman to be proactive about being stimulated and stimulating their partners.

- Some of the most unique modifications of positions come from being experimental and responding to the moment during sex.

Chapter 8

Advanced Positions

In This Chapter

- The three lying positions
- The two pressing positions
- The agile positions
- The standing positions

Ready for more positions? We hope so. The *Kama Sutra* is a seemingly-endless fountain of possible sex positions. That's why this little book has been circulated for centuries and is known worldwide as the foundation of all sexual knowledge.

We now explore the advanced *Kama Sutra* positions. These positions tend to be more difficult to perform than those in the earlier chapters. They require more agility, strength, balance, and more communication with your partner.

Because these are advanced positions, you'll do better with them if you are turned on—and we mean, *really* turned on. So turned on that you could just scream. For maximum pleasure, you must feel relaxed, turned on, warmed up, and ready to move onto the advanced positions. So if you're ready—On your mark, get set, go!

Variety is the spice of life, and no one knew this better than Vatsyayana. He explains that sexual variety is crucial if you want to create and maintain a healthy and amazing sex life. Variety is also important because all bodies are different, all couples fit together differently, and what we each want sexually can change from day to day and even from moment to moment. As a result, it's important for couples to have access to a variety of positions to accommodate their needs and desires, both as a couple and as individuals.

Cultivating a fun and playful mood is another critical element in having a passionate sex life. When you're having fun and being playful, you're naturally relaxed and focused on enjoying the experience. When you focus on being playful, you are able to concentrate on what you're doing, enjoying yourself from moment to moment rather than being focused on some sexual goal. Remember to enjoy yourself and focus on having as much fun as possible—don't get too bogged down in doing it right.

The Three Lying Positions

If we were trying to be cute and funny we'd mention that the following positions are called the lying positions because they involve lying down, but we'll spare you that witticism. In fact, these positions are called the lying positions because in each the woman starts by lying on her back, with her legs spread open.

Good news: Many women find these positions to be highly pleasurable and explosive because of the depth with which the man can thrust during love-making. Be prepared to have a really great time with the lying positions.

Sexy Play

No *Kama Sutra* passion room would be complete without a variety of fluffy pillows for you to use as props while making love. Pillows are useful to place under the woman's back or buttocks for support, or can be used to alter the positions slightly to make them easier to perform.

Widely Opened Position

In this position, the woman starts by lying on her back. She then raises her hips upward, using her thigh muscles to move her pelvis forward. She then spreads her legs apart. If done properly, the woman's buttocks should be several inches off the bed. Since this position can often be tiring and hard to maintain, the woman should try it for a few seconds and then take a break. She should also focus on breathing deeply to help her relax and focus on enjoying the position. She should not stress or tense her muscles.

The man starts on all fours, with his hands planted outside of her shoulders. He can then easily enter her. One of the advantages of this position is that the couple can deepen the experience by looking into each other's eyes while making love.

The woman can move her hips up and down to alter the intensity and depth of the man's entry into her. She can also use her hands and arms to encircle her lover's body. The man can alter his position by lowering his arms and changing his leg positions.

Yawning Position

This yawning position" is *not* the position you take when your lover bores you—you don't need a guidebook for that! This yawning position provides deep, passionate penetration. If you enjoy intensity, you'll enjoy this position.

Again, the woman starts by lying on her back. This time, however, she raises her legs upward toward the man's body, and then she spreads her legs widely apart.

The man starts in the kneeling position with his knees spread slightly more than shoulder length apart. He then guides himself slowly into her yoni, while doing his best to support her legs with his own thighs (see Figure 8.1).

To create variation in feeling and depth, the woman can raise and lower her thighs. She can also experiment with the speed at which she moves her thighs up and down to change the intensity.

The man can change the position by leaning toward or away from his partner.

For added variety, the man and woman can both use their hands and arms to embrace each other, hold hands, or to use their fingertips to touch the erogenous zones of their partner.

Figure 8.1 *Yawning Position.*

The Position of the Wife of Indra

Indra was a well-known Vedic king. According to Vedic texts, he had a wife well known for her sexual skills. Historical rumor claims that she created the position of the wife of Indra because it greatly pleased her husband. What a woman!

This is one of the most advanced positions in the *Kama Sutra*, so you should give yourself time to learn, practice, and experiment with it. You should also take the time to find the most pleasurable variations to suit your body types, as well as your strength and agility limitations.

In this position the woman starts by lying on her back. She then draws her legs up toward her tummy as far as she can, bends her knees, and places her feet on the man's navel region. The man then enters the yoni with her buttocks pressing against his pelvis (see Figure 8.2).

This is considered advanced because of the stress it puts on the woman's legs and abdominal muscles. This position requires a limber body. So go gently at first and work up to doing this position for longer periods of time.

Figure 8.2 *The Position of the Wife of Indra.*

The Clasping Positions

The term *clasping* actually refers to the woman using her vaginal muscles and thighs to capture the man's lingam inside her yoni and hold it there and squeeze it.

Sexy Play

To help women with the clasping positions, we recommend that women perform exercises to help strengthen their ability to clasp the lingam.

Kegel exercises were developed by gynecologist Dr. Arnold Kegel to help women regain bladder control by strengthening their pelvic muscles. The women he trained also found that these exercises also aided in having more powerful orgasms, and added pleasure and satisfaction during sex.

Women can practice doing Kegel exercises by squeezing their pelvic muscles (the muscles that stop the flow of urine) and relaxing them, over and over. Kegel recommends that women start contracting for three seconds and then work up to holding for ten seconds.

In the next set of positions both the man and the woman keep their legs straight, rigid, and held together as tightly as possible. These positions do not focus on embracing, like many of the earlier positions.

The Outstretched Clasping Position

The outstretched clasping position encompasses two separate techniques. The first works as a gentle loving embrace. The second invokes more intensity and passion. The positions work perfectly together, fitting together like puzzle pieces.

In part one, the woman starts out lying on her back with her legs spread open. The man lies on top of her with his body fully extended so that his entire body is on top hers. His legs should also be spread out slightly inside of her legs. The man then slowly and gently moves his lingam inside her yoni (see Figure 8.3).

The woman can arch her legs up slightly to change the angle and pressure of his lingam inside her yoni. The man can alter the intensity and the angle of this position by experimenting with how he moves and positions his legs.

In part two, both partners shift to lying onto their sides facing each other. The man should lie on his left side, and the woman should lie on her right side. We recommend that the man and woman embrace, wrapping their arms around each other and holding each other tightly.

Figure 8.3 *Outstretched Clasping Position.*

For most couples, balancing during this position can be difficult enough, without thinking of adding in any special variations or sexy upgrades. In fact, just trying to find a way to balance in this position might be all the variation most of us can stand. If, however, you do want more variety, the man can vary his style from deep pelvic thrusts to shallow ones.

The Pressing Position

Perform this next position when you are in the heat of passion. If you're not completely burning up and red hot with desire for each other, do not even attempt to try this. But if you are, read on!

The *Kama Sutra* brilliantly observes that love-making moves through different phases from start to finish. Some positions are designed to assist in getting turned on, some for enjoying one another, and some for helping you reach orgasm. This position is designed to be one that pushes both man and woman closer to orgasm, and then over the edge. Here's how it's done: After the couple has been in the clasping position for a while, the woman pushes her thighs tightly together, and presses her pelvis into her partner's pelvis as hard as she can. He thrusts back as hard as he can. As you can imagine, this can be intensely pleasurable.

For variety, the woman can focus on rhythmically tightening and loosening her thighs. The man can also alter this position by rubbing her clitoris or by touching her other erogenous zones.

The Twining Position

Women, you're going to enjoy the twining position because it puts you in charge of the lovemaking.

The twining position is a variation of the pressing position. In this variation, the woman moves one of her legs over the top of one of the man's thighs. At the same time she wraps her arms around the man's neck. By moving her legs and arms, she can experiment with the depth of her lover's penetration.

The woman controls all variation in this position. She can experiment with altering her leg position to change both the sensations and the depth of the lovemaking. She can also use her pelvic muscles to change the angle and intensity of the penetration.

The Rising Position

In the heat of passion, the rising position can be explosive. In this position the man kneels with his knees spread slightly more than shoulder length apart. The woman starts by laying on her back and then lifts her legs up and wraps her feet around the man's neck (see Figure 8.4). He can then easily guide himself inside her.

Figure 8.4 *The Rising Position.*

For variety the man can use his hands to rub her clitoris, caress her breasts, or kiss circles around her lips and tongue.

The woman also can use her hands to rub the man's buttocks, massage his testicles, and use her legs to pull the man closer to her.

The Two Presses

In both pressed positions the woman starts on her back and the man starts by kneeling on top of her. The difference between the two is a change in the woman's leg position. The different leg positions will cause the man's lingam to enter her yoni at different angles.

The Full-Pressed Position

In the full-pressed position, the woman starts on her back. She then raises her legs toward her chest and presses her feet into the man's upper chest.

The man begins in kneeling position with his legs extended slightly more than shoulder length apart (see Figure 8.5). In this position, he can deeply penetrate her yoni.

The woman can change the intensity by pushing her feet harder or softer into the man's chest. The harder she pushes with her feet, the more intense the contractions will be in her pelvis and yoni.

Figure 8.5 *Full Pressed.*

The Half-Pressed Position

In this modification of the full-pressed position, the woman again starts on her back. The man begins in the kneeling position. This time, however, she only places one of her feet on the man's chest. She takes her other leg and wraps it around his waist (see Figure 8.6).

Figure 8.6   *Half Pressed.*

For variety, the woman can pull the man closer to her. This will change the angle at which his lingam is inside her yoni. The man can also change her angle to alter the intensity and sensation.

The Agile Positions

The next group of positions are referred to as the agile positions because they require flexibility and agility to perform. While you do not need yogic flexibility or strength, they are more difficult than most positions in this book. So take your time, go slowly, and enjoy.

The Splitting of Bamboo

Once again, another strange sounding name for a hot sex position. Fortunately, the splitting of bamboo is not a cleverly disguised *Kama Sutra* "code word" for something that means "this is really painful." In fact, the name of this position simply refers to the leg positions of the man and woman. It is another highly pleasurable position.

The woman starts on her back, with her legs bent (much like she would in the traditional missionary position). The man begins in the kneeling position with both of his hands placed on either side of her head, near her ears. The woman then raises one leg and places it over one of his shoulders. At the same time, she takes her other leg and rests it on the bed (see Figure 8.7).

Figure 8.7   *Splitting of Bamboo.*

The woman alternates her resting and outstretched legs. The man, in turn, also alternates extending one of his legs forward and one backward, as the woman switches leg positions.

The Fixing of a Nail

In this position the woman starts by laying on her back with her legs outstretched—similar to the splitting of bamboo position. The man starts out in the kneeling position with his knees slightly wider than his shoulders. The woman then takes one of her legs and raises it toward the man's head. She then rests her heel on his forehead (see Figure 8.8).

The advantage to this position is that, with her leg extended so high in the air, the woman feels an added sense of vulnerability and sensuality in this position.

For variety, the man can change the angle at which he kneels on top of the woman. This change can greatly alter the sensations for the lovers and also alter the depth at which his lingam penetrates her yoni.

The woman can also intensify her experience by pushing harder or more softly into the man's forehead. Be warned: Don't push into his forehead too hard; you might just knock him out.

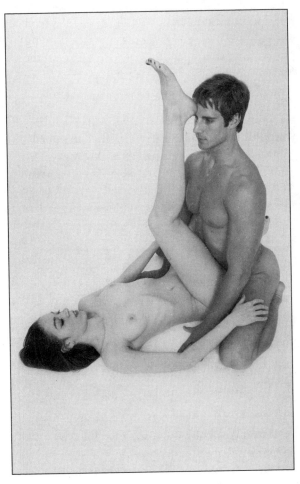

Figure 8.8 *Fixing of a Nail.*

The Crab's Position

Why is this position named after a crab, you ask? Believe it or not, the woman's yoni acts like a crab, tightly gripping the man's lingam during sex. There you have it—what could be more obvious?

The crab's position starts with the man kneeling with his knees widely spread apart. The woman starts on her back and then draws her legs toward her stomach. She then wraps her legs around the man's waist. He then bends slightly toward her, but mainly focuses on keeping his back straight and his body as still as possible (see Figure 8.9).

The variation in this position all comes from the woman. She can move her pelvis into different angles when she wraps her legs around his waist.

The Packed Position

The man starts by kneeling with his knees bent slightly more than shoulder length apart, so that his feet extend behind his body. The woman again starts on her back. She then raises her legs toward her chest. Next, she crosses her feet so that they make an "x" shape, and presses them into the man's upper chest. The man then has easy access to her yoni and can go very deeply inside her. He can also caress her buttocks and breasts.

Figure 8.9   *The Crab's Position.*

The Lotus-Like Position

In Hindu culture, the lotus is a symbol of perfect unity and union. The Lotus-like position is based on the idea of perfect harmony between men and women.

The woman starts out on her back. She then draws her legs toward her body. She then takes one leg at a time and folds it over her opposite thigh. The man begins crouching on top of the woman on all fours (see Figure 8.10). The man can then gently slide his lingam inside her yoni.

The lotus position can be quite tiring for the woman's legs and back. Try this position for short periods of time at first, and gradually work up to longer sessions.

Tidbits of Pleasure

Have you ever wondered how the yogis get into the full lotus position? You probably haven't, but we're going to tell you anyway.

Sit on the floor with your back straight and legs stretched out in front of you, slightly apart. Place right foot on the left thigh with the sole of the foot turned up. Rest your right knee on the ground. Take left foot and place it high on the right thigh with the sole facing up and the left knee resting on the ground. Let your feet rest on the pressure points at the top of your groin.

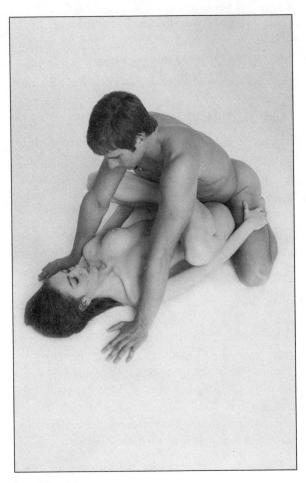

Figure 8.10 *The Lotus-Like Position.*

For variety, the woman can change the angle at which she is holding her legs. Altering the angle can change the sensation and depth in which the lingam penetrates the yoni.

The Standing Unions

Ready for yet another crazy variety of sex positions? This time the *Kama Sutra* recommends you do it while standing up! Talk about variety. Here goes with a variety of standing positions.

The Supported Congress

In the supported congress you both begin standing up. Hug each other. Embrace each other. Kiss each other. Look deeply into each other's eyes and breathe in union for a minute or so.

The man starts by standing with his back supported against a wall. The woman wraps one her legs around one of the man's legs (see Figure 8.11). He then carefully proceeds to enter her yoni. The woman must focus on keeping her balance during this position so that she can enjoy the experience rather than toppling to the floor.

To make the position easier, the man can squat down to lower his body to meet her yoni. We recommend the man grab and support the woman's buttocks during the position to aid in her comfort.

Figure 8.11   *Supported Congress.*

The Suspended Congress

In this position the man stands with his back against a wall. The woman begins by wrapping her arms around his neck. She then supports her inner thighs on his hip bones. The man reaches down and grabs her legs, thus supporting her body with the strength of his arms (see Figure 8.12).

Figure 8.12 *Suspended Congress.*

For most men this position is difficult to maintain
for any length of time. Obviously, you need to have
a lot of upper body strength to hold a woman in
that position. Be careful when trying this position
and be willing to start and stop, combining it with
other positions.

The Least You Need to Know

- In your sex life, make sure you experiment
  and utilize a variety of positions, postures,
  and methods of lovemaking.

- You should have fun and enjoy making
  love with your partner.

- If something doesn't feel good, stop and
  alter the position to best suit your body
  types.

- Sex is best when the partners take turns
  giving and receiving pleasure.

Chapter 9

Beginning and Ending Positions

In This Chapter

- Positions to use at the begging of the lovemaking process
- The four "animal" positions
- The four types of loving congress
- Positions to intensify passion throughout the lovemaking process

You can use the positions in this chapter at any point in lovemaking (of course, you don't need our permission for that!), but they are especially good at the beginning, when your lovemaking is just revving up, or near the end, when your lovemaking is reaching its climax.

You naturally make changes in your lovemaking positions based on how far you are into the lovemaking session: At the beginning of lovemaking, for instance, a particularly excited man is likely to make adjustments to slow down his excitement and help the session last longer. Either partner, when nearing climax, will naturally speed up and make other adjustments in thrusting, speed, angles, and so on, to bring the union to completion. A single position can, in fact, be a variety of positions, depending upon the small adjustments the lovers make as they proceed.

The Four "Animal" Positions

Part of the genius of Vatsyayana, which he brought to the *Kama Sutra*, is that he recognized simple sexual positions and built upon them. He saw that a rear-entry position, for instance, was fundamentally different at the beginning of lovemaking, when the partners are proceeding slowly and making eye contact, than it is at the end of the session.

This is good news to all who have felt bad about the apparent lack of variety in their otherwise good sex life. Some couples' only problem is that they've felt that something must be lacking in their sex lives because they only used two or three (admittedly very satisfying) positions. Once they realize that there is tremendous variety and intimacy available in the positions they do use, they feel much better about their sex lives.

The Congress of a Cow

The *congress* of a cow is simpler, more fun, and far less insulting than it sounds. This is a standing, rear-entry position. The woman stands with her legs straight and slightly apart. She bends at the waist and places her hands on the floor in front of her. The man, standing behind her, enters her from behind (see Figure 9.1).

Kama Sutra Words

Congress is not meant to refer to the legislature of the United States. Congress in The *Kama Sutra* refers to a sexual position, just as "union" also referred to a sexual position.

This position makes very deep penetration possible. It is not ideally suited for women whose yonis are shorter than the lingam of their lover.

Like all rear-entry positions, the congress of the cow can be an excellent position in which to stimulate the woman's G-spot. It's a good idea to experiment with a variety of rear-entry positions to see which one accomplishes this best.

Not every woman is flexible enough to comfortably place her hands on the floor in front of her. The woman can rest her hands, or her folded arms and head, on a pillow, on a chair, on the arm of a couch, or on a table or bed, if needed.

Figure 9.1 *Congress of a Cow.*

In this position the man has a lot of control over the speed and momentum of the lovemaking. This can lead to him climaxing before the woman is ready. If the woman senses this is happening and wants to extend the lovemaking, she should tell him that she'd like to do a different position for a while. The lovers can then return to this position at the end of the lovemaking session.

The man's experience of this position will change as he experiments with different ways of holding his lover's body as he thrusts. The man will find he gets different types of penetration and sensation as he varies grasping her by her thighs, hips, and waist.

The man can also use his hands to caress the woman's buttocks, back, breasts, and hips in this position. The man can experiment with reaching around the woman with one hand and stimulating her clitoris in time with the thrusting.

If you start with this position, you may want to transition next to the congress of a dog.

The Congress of a Dog

This is the most commonly used rear-entry posture, typically called "doggy-style." The woman kneels with her hands and knees on the floor or bed and her legs somewhat spread. The man kneels behind her and enters her from behind, with his knees between her knees, gripping her by her waist.

The woman then turns her head to gaze into the eyes of her lover (see Figure 9.2).

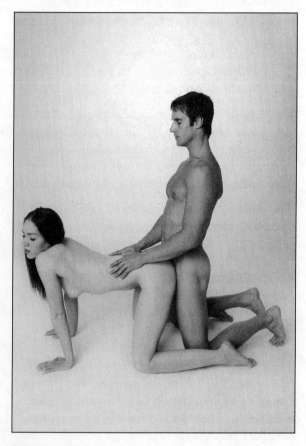

Figure 9.2 *Congress of a Dog.*

This position is excellent for deep, hard penetration and for G-spot stimulation. The man should try varying how much he pushes upward and downward as you both press together and draw apart. That will help you discover together which type of thrust makes best contact with the woman's G-spot.

The woman turns her head to make eye contact with the man to increase the intimacy and tenderness of the position. If this is awkward or uncomfortable, place a mirror in front of the woman's face, and use it to see each other's eyes and faces.

This position gives the woman more control over the speed and depth of the thrusts than she has in the congress of a cow. She can make use of that by altering her speed and varying how hard she thrusts backward to meet the man's thrusting.

It is also easy for the woman to pleasure her own clitoris during the sex, or to fondle her partner's scrotum.

Sometimes a woman kneeling in the congress of the dog will seem too low toward the bed or too high to easily enter. Remember, you are allowed (and even encouraged!) to communicate during sex. Try spreading your knees wider to accommodate each other's stance, or feel free to ask your partner to either bring his or her knees slightly together, or to spread them more apart.

Because the congress of a dog facilitates deep, hard penetration, don't use this if the man tends to climax easily, unless you are nearing the end of lovemaking. If the position is too intense early in your lovemaking, feel free to shift to some other position.

The Congress of a Deer

The congress of a dog will often transition into the congress of a deer. When you transition from the dog to the deer, you will notice that the sense of tender intimacy gives way to more passionate, aggressive lovemaking.

From the Master

Here's how *Kama Sutra* translator Indra Sinha describes the congress of a deer:

"If the lady, eager for love,
Goes on all fours, humping her back like a doe,
And you enjoy her from behind,
Rutting as though you'd lost all human nature,
It is 'the deer.'"

You and your partner may find it pleasurable to intentionally transition back and forth between the dog and the deer, building the passion until you find yourself in the deer, purposefully slowing down, and transitioning back into the dog. In this way you can use the *Kama Sutra* as it was intended; to create variety and greatly increased sexual pleasure through intentional choices.

The Pressing of an Elephant

We apologize for these unattractive names. The *Kama Sutra* is clear in saying that each animal has its own method of lovemaking that human lovers can copy. He does not mean these names to be an assessment of anyone's personal attractiveness. The pressing of an elephant, indeed!

This position is very simple: The woman lies flat on her stomach with her legs straight and close together, with her hips slightly flexed, to facilitate easier entry for the man. The man lies flat over her, supporting himself on his arms, and enters her. His legs are outside of, but touching, her legs (see Figure 9.3). This position benefits from full-body contact. A sense of closeness is achieved by the large amount of skin-to-skin contact provided by the man lying so fully on top of the woman.

Paying attention to the details of your touching can add a lot to this posture. Lovers may touch their feet to one another's feet, or interlace their fingers to add erotic, sensitive detail.

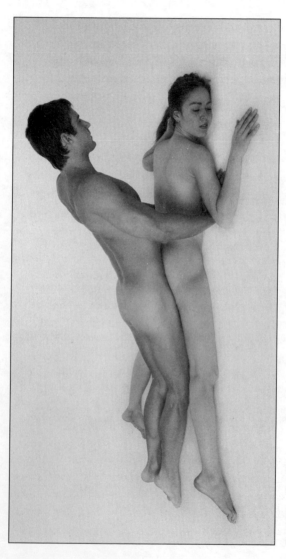

Figure 9.3 *Pressing of an Elephant.*

It may be easier for the man to enter the woman, and be more pleasurable for her, if you put a pillow or cushion under her hips to raise her buttocks slightly.

The woman can improve the experience for both herself and her lover by pressing her thighs together once he has entered her—this creates a delicious tightness, as well as providing more stimulation to his scrotum as he presses into the woman.

The woman can facilitate deeper penetration by pressing her buttocks against the man as he thrusts into her.

If the man bends his knees a little and tucks his pelvis, it will be easier to achieve deep penetration.

The man should use his arms to support himself, but he should touch his chest to the woman's back. The man should be conscious about how much weight he puts on his partner's back while he is thrusting into her.

The Four Types of Loving Congress

Life is full of many types of experiences. Loving is no different. Sometimes the feelings, sensations, and experiences you have during lovemaking are transcendent, ecstatic, or spiritual. If you know what to look for, you can see and savor these experiences as they come your way.

Here are the four types of lovemaking described by the *Kama Sutra:*

The Congress of Subsequent Love

The congress of subsequent love is the experience of lovemaking when the love is new.

Too often in our modern world, men and women who are infatuated with one another rush into having sex before they know each other very well. They have sex the first time they are physical with one another, rather than building up to it over time.

We don't think this is bad, but we do want to point out this possibility: You have exactly one opportunity to get to know your lover for the first time. Early in your relationship is the only time when you and your partner will experience the newness of the congress of subsequent love, and the newness of exploring and discovering each other for the first time. If you let yourself be aware of the congress of subsequent love when it comes your way, you will be able to slow down and savor it all the more.

The Loving Congress

Loving congress is the experience of lovemaking after some sort of a separation. Perhaps you've been separated by one of you being on a journey, or you live far from one another, and it's been difficult to get together. Or perhaps the separation was psychological; you had a fight or quarrel, and now have made up, and want to make love. Such lovemaking is loving congress.

When you experience loving congress after a separation, be sure to pay attention to those reuniting feelings during the lovemaking. They are special, and unusual, and worthy of note when they appear.

During this type of lovemaking, allow yourself to notice and bask in the good feelings of reuniting. Such feelings can't be faked or called forth on demand. Noticing when you are reuniting with loving congress will allow you to really treasure those sensations.

Loving congress is similar to the congress of subsequent love in that there is a newness present, when you return to your lover after an absence. The *Kama Sutra* reminds us to experience and enjoy that quality of newness when it is available to us.

The Congress of Transferred Love

The congress of transferred love is sex during which the man fantasizes about being with someone else. In our modern world, the congress of transferred love applies as much to women's wandering imaginations as it does to men's.

Sexy Play

Sex in the bathtub can be great, if done right—the warm water, the soap suds, the hot feeling of your lover's body pressed against you as you writhe hard together.

Here are the important things to keep in mind when having sex in water:

- **Lubrication:** Water tends to wash away a woman's natural lubrication, so you'll want to have some other type of silicon-based lubrication on hand to keep things moving.

- **Be ready for some awkwardness:** Most bathtubs are not designed for sex, so be willing to be patient through some awkwardness as you get yourselves positioned.

- **Use variety:** Standing sex while showering can be very erotic, as can oral sex in the bath.

Having some fantasies about partners other than your own is natural, and in itself nothing to worry about. The main purpose of the *Kama Sutra* is to help couples keep their relationships alive by providing ways of varying lovemaking, keeping it so interesting and so exciting that the occasional

fantasy about another partner doesn't become
an obsession that can ruin a relationship.

The Congress of Spontaneous Love

The congress of spontaneous love is the normal,
everyday lovemaking that couples do, naturally and
spontaneously. It is a pleasurable way to reaffirm
and deepen the attachment between you and your
partner. As you and your lover practice the *Kama
Sutra* positions in this book, your congress of spontaneous love will become better and better.

The Least You Need to Know

- Change the intensity when you are near
  the beginning and just revving up, or near
  the end, when the lovemaking is reaching
  its climax.

- Men need to stay conscious of a woman's
  orgasm cycle and focus on her pleasure
  during the lovemaking process.

- Remember, stroking your lover's hair, rubbing his or her feet, and playing with your
  partner's genitals all add to the process.

- Listen to your partner's fantasies, share
  your fantasies, and communicate with
  other to create safety and intimacy in your
  relationship.

Chapter 10

Beyond Total Satisfaction

In This Chapter

- Tips on integrating the *Kama Sutra* into everyday life
- Why focusing on the "little details" in both sexuality and developing intimacy is essential
- How to keep your romantic life vital and healthy
- How to develop a lifelong relationship based on intimacy, passion, and vitality

How to Integrate the *Kama Sutra* into Your Life

While the *Kama Sutra* is, at its basic level, about sex, it's actually a doorway into much, much more.

Your sexuality is about your life. It's a microcosm of your experience of this world as a physical body. The more skill you develop in being aware of and enjoying direct physical experience during sex, the more aware, present, calm, and peaceful you'll be in your day-to-day life.

Fundamentally the *Kama Sutra* advises you to pay attention to what you are doing during lovemaking. It inspires you to let go of rote, automatic, or habitual sexuality, and to embrace the complete newness of each sexual experience you have.

Being able to access this level of awareness will serve you in every area of your life. Imagine being able to go about your life fully aware of your surroundings, unhurried, at peace, and able to fully experience and fully enjoy each moment. This is what the *Kama Sutra* offers you.

To that end, it makes sense to think about *Kama Sutra* practices, methods, and distinctions as you go about your day. Here are some *Kama Sutra*–inspired ways you can practice bringing sensual awareness to everything you do:

- **Practice being unhurried.** For part of each day, let go of all sense of urgency or hurry. Allow activities to take as long as they take. Let go of resisting inconveniences or things that slow you down, and simply be present.

- **Add romantic details to every area of your life.** The *Kama Sutra* tells us that sensuality is in the details of life, and there's no reason to limit your use of this fact to your sex life. If you are taking a bath, light some candles. If you are spending some time reading, put on some mood music. If you are cooking food, go the extra distance to make the meal special in some way. The more you can bring romantic details into every area of your life, the more *Kama Sutra* sensuality will be available to you at all times.

- **Notice and enjoy the little things in life.** Similarly, noticing and enjoying the little things will bring a *Kama Sutra* consciousness into your everyday life. Enjoy the beauty of a tree, or a cloud, or a work of art. Let the little things in life delight you on a daily basis and you will integrate the *Kama Sutra* even more.

- **Continuously refine the art of sensual living.** Socializing with others, cooking good food, playing music and games, making your home beautiful—all of these activities will increase your sensual experience of life and are worth pursuing.

How to Keep Your Relationships Healthy and Vital

Sexuality is a key—but only one of the keys a good relationship requires. Being good at love-making is not enough to sustain a relationship through the ups and downs that all romantic partnerships must endure. At the same time, healthy sexuality is a powerful relationship glue that can help hold two people together if other key aspects of relating are also in place. A good, healthy, long lasting relationship includes a strong sexual connection.

Here are some other simple, yet, vital parts of a good relationship:

- **Appreciation of one another.** If the *Kama Sutra* tells us one thing about lovemaking, it's that appreciating and enjoying your lover as much as possible is an extremely good idea. Just as couples tend to fall into sexual ruts, they also fall into ruts of lack of appreciation.

  Fortunately this problem is easy to fix. When you see something about your lover you could admire, admire it. Let him or her know that you think that she is great, and why. This will build

your relationship connection just as enjoying
and appreciating each other in bed builds
your sexual connection.

- **Doing the little things.** Just as you must
  pay attention to the little sensual details in
  lovemaking, you must also pay attention
  to the little details in your relationship.
  Doing the little things can be exceedingly
  simple, and even fun, and make a huge difference in the level of emotional bonding
  in a relationship.

If you appreciate each other and focus on the little
things in your relationship—just as the *Kama Sutra*
would have you do in your sexuality—you will start
to build up an emotional bank account of good feelings and high regard for one another. Each time
you appreciate your partner, and each time you do a
little thing for him or her, you will be making a
deposit into that account.

When your relationship does encounter hard times
(as all of them do), this bank account will serve as a
cushion that will allow you to stay together, communicate, forgive, and cut each other some slack as
you might need to. You will have built up so much
emotional goodwill that you both will naturally
desire to make the relationship work. In this way,
the work you do in a relationship during the good

times—appreciating and doing the little things—can carry you through the bad times. And that is important.

Although the *Kama Sutra* is about lovemaking, it's worth remembering that, when you have a relationship based on appreciation and the little things, all aspects of your relationship can be an experience of lovemaking.

We suggest you allow your practice of the *Kama Sutra* to spread into your life in the ways we've described in this chapter. You can have sexual satisfaction, and beyond—so take advantage of this guide, and experience every aspect of your life at a whole new level.

And remember, you can get more *Kama Sutra* tips e-mailed to you by simply sending a blank e-mail to tips@passionatekamasutra.com or by visiting www.passionatekamasutra.com.

We wish you all the best in your new sexual adventures! All of your relationship can be lovemaking.

The Least You Need to Know

- Add romantic details to every area of your life.
- A healthy sex and sensual life will aid in building lifelong intimacy and connection in your relationship.

- Open and honest communication is vital both in the bedroom as well in every other area of your life.
- Continuously refine the art of sensual living.

Index

M

N

O

Y–Z